MW00882370

The A320 pilot book

Author: Victor Diaz

Book cover: Carlos Diaz

ISBN - 9798645275990

Barcelona, Spain — 2020 (Edition 2.0)

About the author

I am a Spanish First Officer with over 4000 A320 hours. I graduated from CTC Wings (in the UK) in 2014 being a Monarch cadet. After that, I moved to a British orange airline and now to a yellow colored airline based in my home city. Besides flying, I am a translator and interpreter and I love writing too.

Note: "Monarch" is used as a callsign in some examples as a tribute to my first and extinct airline.

Changes Control (From Edition 1.5 to 2.0)

Minor aesthetic modifications.

New content added in Sections 5 (new tables and graphs), 9 (circuit breakers, commercial P/B), 10 (new graph for the flight controls — hydraulics schematics), 15 (new ADIRU information, new TO config button information), 18 (G/A procedure, upset recovery information modified), 21 (V_{app} calculation) and 23 (cockpit emergency equipment).

Major changes in Chapter 17, including a whole new paragraph regarding TCAS. Addition of OEB57.

Disclaimer:

This book is for training purposes only.

This is an unofficial document, not approved by Airbus SE

"Airbus" and "A320" are registered trademarks belonging to Airbus SE

No responsibility is taken for mistakes or omissions

Official documents (FCOM, OM, FCTM...) are the final authority.

Contact me

Something to say? Inputs? Suggestions? Found any mistakes or omissions?

✉ flying.quill89@gmail.com

1. INTRODUCTION

NOTE: Numbers next to the titles are the FCOM chapter for that particular item.

1. INTRODUCTION

The A320 Pilot Book is designed to be the all-you-need book for your day to day operations as well as for your sim checks. It lets you have all you need in a single book. It contains:

- A320 knowledge (systems with schematics, abnormal operations, OEB)
- Basic ATPL theory (performance, meteorology, law)
- Operational knowledge (failure management, walk around, MEL...)

However, in this book you will **not** find:

- Normal procedures (as they heavily vary from airline to airline)
- Handling skills
- FMGC set up

You will even find a Chapter 25 all for yourself, designed to take notes from your SIM sessions or maybe add some more information.

Even if designed for professional pilots, the A320 pilot book can also be used via type rating students, ATPL holders applying for a job or aviation enthusiasts.

BIBLIOGRAPHY

The following books have been used as a reference:

- *FCOM, FCTM, AFM, MEL*; Airbus
- *Aircraft Characteristics Airport And Maintenance Planning,* Airbus
- *Getting to grips* (different topics), Airbus
- *EASA Professional Pilot Studies*, Phil Croucher
- ACE the Technical Pilot Interview, Gary Bristow
- *Aviation Exam* (Performance, Meteorology)
- *The A320 Study Guide*

ABREVIATIONS

A/C	Aircraft
A/SKID	Anti-skid
A/THR	Autothrust
ABCU	Alt. Brake Control Unit
ABN	Abnormal
ACM	Air Cycle Machine
ACP	Audio Control Panel
ADIRS	Air Data Inertail Reference System
ADIRU	Air Data Inertial Reference Unit
ADM	Air Data Module
ADR	Air Data Reference
ALT	Altitude
AP	Autopilot
APU	Auxiliary Power Unit
BCL	Battery Charge Limiter
BMC	Bleed Monitoring Computer
BRK	Brake
BSCU	Brakes Steering Control Unit
BTC	Bus Tie Connector
C/L	Checklist
CDLS	Cockpit Door Locking Sys.
CFDS	Centralized Fault Display Sys.
CIDS	Cabin Intercommunication Data System
CKPT	Cockpit
CPC	Cabin Pressure Controller
CPT	Captain
CVR	Cockpit Voice Recorder
DMC	Display Management Compute

DMU	Data Management Unit
DU	Display Unit
ECB	Electronic Control Box
ECU	Engine Control Unit
EDP	Engine Driven Pump
EEC	Electronic Engine Computer
EFIS	Electronic Flight Instrument Sys
EFOB	Estimated Fuel On Board
EIU	Engine Interface Unit
EMER	Emergency
EO	Engine Out
ESS	Essential
F/O	First Officer
FAC	Flight Augmentation Computer
FADEC	Full Authority Digital Engine Control
FAP	Forward Attendant Panel
FAV	Fan Air Valve
FCU	Flight Control Unit
FD	Flight Director
FF	Fuel Flow
FMA	Flight Mode Annunciator
FMU	Fuel Metering Unit
FWC	Flight Warning Computer
FWS	Flight Warning System
GCU	Generator Control Unit
GLC	Generator Line Contractor
HDG	Heading
HMU	Hydromechanical Unit
HP	High Pressure
IDG	Integrated Drive Generator
IGN	Ignition
IP	Intermediate Pressure

IRS	Inertial Reference System		RMP	Radio Management Panel
ISPSS	In-Seat Power Supply System		RNP	Required Navigation Performance
kt	Knot			
L/G	Landing Gear		SBY	Standby
LAF	Load Alleviation Function		SDAC	System Data Acquisition Concentrator
LGCIU	Landing Gear Control Interface Unit			
			SEC	Spoiler Elevator Computer
LNAV	Lateral Navigation		SFCC	Slat/Flap Control Computer
LVL	Level		SPD	Speed
MCDU	Multi purpose Control Unit and Display		STS	Status
			SW	Switch
MDA	Minimum Descent Altitude		THR	Thrust
MSA	Minimum Safe Altitude		THS	Trimmable Horizontal Stabilizer
N/W	Nose wheel		TLA	Thrust Lever Angle
ND	Navigation Display		TR	Transformer Rectifier
NWS	Nose Wheel Steering		V/DEV	Vertical Deviation
OM	Operations Manual		VHF	Very High Frequency
P/B	Pushbutton		V_{LE}	Extended Gear Speed Limit
PAX	Passenger		V_{LO}	Operating Gear Speed Limit
PBE	Protect Breathing Equipment		V_{LS}	Lowest Selectable Speed
PF	Pilot Flying		VNAV	Vertical Navigation
PFD	Primary Flight Display		WAI	Wing Anti-Ice
PM	Pilot Monitoring		WHC	Window Heat Computer
PTT	Push to Talk		WTB	Wing Tip Brake
PTU	Power Transfer Unit		WX	Weather
QRH	Quick Reference Handbook		XFR	Transfer
RAT	Ram Air Turbine		XTK	Cross track
RCL	Recall			

2. BASICS — PERFORMANCE AND PRINCIPLES OF FLIGHT

Lift

Lift is the phenomenon generated by an airfoil due to pressure differences above and below it. The following formula explains lift generation:

$$L = \tfrac{1}{2}\rho v^2 S C_L$$

Where:

- ○ ρ (*rho*): density
- ○ v: true airspeed
- ○ S: wing surface
- ○ C_L: coefficient of lift

Drag

Drag is the difference in static pressure across a plane perpendicular to the flight path, which tends to slow down the aircraft. There are different kinds of drag:

- Induced drag: appears when lift is created. Air at different pressures mixes at the wingtip, producing vortices near it. These vortices are unstable and change the speed and the direction of the wind flow in the trailing edge, inducing downwash (drag) behind the wing.
- Parasite drag: comes from anything moving through the air that is not actually creating lift, like the undercarriage.

Lift/Drag ratio

The airspeed where drag is minimum can be seen from a graph that compares total to parasite and induced drag:

 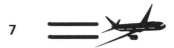

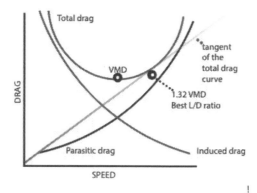

As you can see, as airspeed increases parasite drag increases too, and as airspeed reduces, induced drag decreases.

At the bottom of the graph we find **V$_{MD}$**, that is, the minimum drag speed. The best lift/drag ratio speed is found where the tangent of the total drag curve meets the curve, which happens at speeds higher than V$_{MD}$ (1.32).

The speed range below L/D$_{MAX}$ (left of the curve) in a jet is the *speed unstable regime*. Drag increases as you slow down so power must be added in order to maintain slower speeds.

Endurance and range

For a jet A/C, max A/C endurance is achieved at VMD (bottom of the drag curve), whereas MAX Range is achieved at 1.32 VMD.

Centre of Gravity...

is the point through which the total body of the A/C will act.

Centre of Pressure...

is a theoretical point on the chord line through which the resultant of all forces is said to act, so the sum of all moments there is zero. It is normally found around 25 % of the way from the leading edge.

Aerodynamic Center...

is the fixed point on the chord line about which changes in pitching moments are constant when the angle of attack changes. However, it does move when you get supersonic.

Aspect Ratio...

is the relationship between its length and width. The higher it is, the less induced drag you get.

Angle of attack

Is an aerodynamic angle between the chord line and the relative wind.

Speeds

Indicated airspeed (IAS): is the direct reading corrected only for instrument error.

Calibrated airspeed (CAS): is the IAS corrected for pressure errors, which are highest at low speeds

Equivalent airspeed (EAS): is the CAS compensated for comprensibility, or factors arising from high speeds.

True airspeed (TAS): is the CAS corrected for altitude and temperature or density. In ISA conditions at sea level, CAS = TAS. On average, TAS increases by 2 % over IAS for every 1000 ft.

Mach number...

is a true airspeed indication given as a percentage relative to the local speed of sound.

M_{crit} is the aircraft's Mach at which the airflow over a wing become sonic. At that point, the aircraft experiences:

- o   Mach buffet caused by shockwaves on the wing's upper surface
- o   Increase in drag
- o   Nose-down change in attitude (Mach tuck)
- o   Possible loss of control

Coffin corner

The coffin corner is an aircraft's absolute ceiling, where Mach number buffet and pre-stall buffet are coincident.

Absolute/maximum service ceiling

The absolute ceiling is a point where the aircraft has no excess of power and only one speed allows to fly steady and level flight. That range in which the aircraft flies is the abovementioned coffin corner.

The service ceiling is a maximum operating altitude or flight level where the best rate of climb will produce 500 feet-per-minute in clean configuration with maximum power.

Range and endurance

Range is the distance an aircraft can fly on a given amount of fuel and endurance the time it can remain in flight. Both are related to engine fuel consumption, which varies depending on the engine type and altitude.

ENDURANCE				RANGE			
Speed	Weight	height	wind	Speed	Weight	height	wind
V_{MD}	↓	↑	No effect	1.32 V_{MD}	↓	↑	Head↓ Tail ↑

Rate and angle of climb

The rate of climb (ROC) is the A/C vertical speed.

Vy is indicated as the speed for the best rate of climb. It allows the pilot to maximize altitude gain per time.

Vx is indicated at the speed for the best angle of climb. It allows the pilot to maximize altitude gain per horizontal distance. For a jet A/C, this happens at V_{MD}.

Increase	Climb angle	ROC	Vx	Vy	TODA
height	↓	↓	↑	IAS ↓ TAS ↑	↑
temperature	↓	↓	↑	↓	↑
weight	↓	↓	↑	↑	↑
flap	↓	↓	↓	↓	↓

Critical point...

Also known as equal-time point, is the enroute track position where it is quicker to go your destination than to go back. Is calculated as follows:

Distance to CP = DH / (O+H)

D: total sector distance

H: ground speed home

O: ground speed out

Point of no return...

is the last point on a route at which it is possible to return to the departure aerodrome with a sensible fuel reserve.

Time to PNR = EH / (O x H)

E: Safe endurance time

H: ground speed home

O: ground speed out

TAKE-OFF AND LANDING DISTANCES

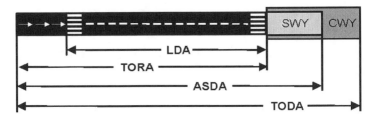

SWY: Stopway: area beyond the end of the TORA which is prepared for an airplane to stop in the event of an abandoned T/O.
CWY: Clearway: Area provided beyond the TORA that is free from objects that may cause hazard to airplanes in flight.

TORA

Take-off run available, which is the declared available runway length for take off.

TODA

Take-off distance available. The take off distance is calculated from brake release to a screen height of 35 ft for jet airplanes. Screen height is 15 ft for wet runways.

ASDA

The Accelerate Stop Distance (ASD) is calculated from A/C acceleration to V1, then a 2s recognition time, and then a full stop. ASDA is the length of the take off run available plus the length of the stopway available.

LDA

The length of the runway which is declared available by the authority and suitable for the ground run of a landing airplane.

ALD

Actual Landing Distance, which is the horizontal distance necessary to come to a complete stop from a point 50 ft above the RUNWAY. ALD is demonstrated a in a flight test carried out in certain conditions (ISA conditions, no reverse credited... etc).

LDR

Is the demonstrated Actual Landing Distance, multiplied by:

- 1.67 for DRY runways
- 1.92 for WET runways

PERFORMANCE GRADIENTS

Landing Climb Requirement — Landing flaps, gear down, AEO at go-around thrust. Climb gradient shall not be less than 3,2 % with a speed of 1.23 VS.

Approach Climb Requirement — Approach flaps, gear up, OEI with remaining engine at G/A thrust. Speed shall be 1.5 VS for a minimum gradient of 2,1 % for a two-engine aircraft.

Low visibility Climb — calculated at 2,5 % with the normal speed and configuration used for go around, with one engine inoperative, with decision heights below 200 ft.

TAKE-OFF SEGMENTS

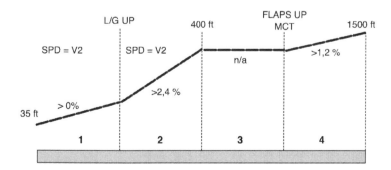

3. BASICS — MET

ISA Conditions

Are a standard of the atmosphere which is accepted as standard for the purposes of calibration and performance. They are:

- temperature: 15ºC, decreasing 1,98ºC every 1000 ft.
- Pressure: 1013,25 hPa, decreasing 1mb every 27 ft.

Instruments only give us accurate information when we are in ISA conditions. Otherwise, they should be corrected for real information.

ATMOSPHERE

In the picture to the right you will be able to see the atmosphere layers and the approximate height of each one of them —although layers' height is variable—.

Temperature within the atmosphere initially falls from around 15º C (ISA conditions) to around -56,5º C on average. Then it rises again through the stratosphere, causing a temperature inversion that stops most of the cloud formation at the tropopause (boundary between the troposphere and the stratosphere).

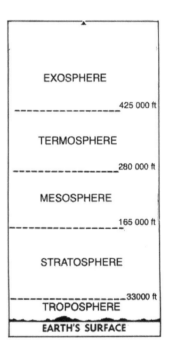

CLOUDS

Clouds are formed when relative humidity reaches 100 % and the air mass becomes saturated. Subsequently, water condenses.

In the picture below you will see a representation of the most common clouds. Of course, the famous **CB** (Cumulonimbus) is the most dangerous for aviation, as it brings thunderstorms that are a source of multiple risks for aircrafts: hail, updrafts and downdrafts, turbulence, severe icing or electrical and magnetic activity amongst them.

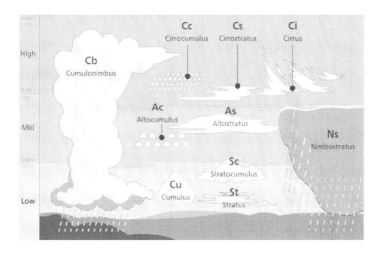

Apart from the ones seen above, two clouds are especially relevant to aviation:

Altocumulus lenticularis:	Altocumulus castellanus
it is caused by mountain waves, normally created downwind of a mountain. Turbulence in this area might become severe.	Its presence is a clear sign of turbulence nearby. Formation of thunderstorms in this area is highly likely.

FOG

There are three different kinds of fog:

Radiation fog: normally occurs inland, especially in valleys. Requires cloudless nights, moist air and light winds.

Advection fog: can occur can suddenly in one of the following situations:

- warm, moist air flowing across a colder surface, which is cooled from below.

- winds encouraging mixing of air resulting in a layer of fog

- sea fog, occurring when very cold air passes over a warmer sea that causes evaporating moisture to condense.

Frontal fog: forming due to the interaction between two air masses, one colder than the other.

WIND...

is the horizontal movement of air, produced by the sun heat and by the Earth rotation. Technically it is defined as the compensation of the difference in atmospheric pressure between two points.

Wind normally goes from High to Low Pressure areas. However, it is affected by the following phenomena:

Coriolis force: is caused by the Earth rotation (around itself). Coriolis force is always perpendicular to the wind vector. In the Northern Hemisphere, this means that Coriolis causes the wind to turn right —opposite effect in the Southern Hemisphere—.

Friction force: When air moves over a surface its speed decreases, especially over land (this effect is weaker over water). The wind will also back (turn anticlockwise) when descending. The effect of friction is negligible above 3000ft.

PRESSURE SYSTEMS

A pressure system is an area of the Earth's atmosphere that has particularly high or low pressure compared to the air surrounding it. There are two main kinds of pressure systems:

Anticyclones — High Pressure systems: The air within them descends in the atmosphere (thus causing the high pressure area over the surface), thus causing quiet, dry and settled weather. Descending air is not always equal to good weather though, as might trap smoke or haze leading to reduced visibility, especially near industrial areas.

Cyclones — Low Pressure systems: The air rises within them, thus causing instability. Instability may lead to convection activity and, eventually, to the generation of thunderstorms. They normally move NE in the Northern Hemisphere, with a speed between 10 to 40 kt, and they normally live for around 4 to 6 days. Fronts normally radiate from the low center.

FRONTS

A front is a transition between two air masses. There are two basic kinds of fronts:

Warm front: this exists where warm air overtakes a colder air mass and is force upwards over it. The first clouds approaching a witness will be high clouds like cirrus, followed by altostratus and then nimbostratus, leaving long lasting rain and drizzle. The temperature will fall as the front passes and the wind will back. One the front has passed, frontal fog will usually be found.

Cold front: this exists where cold dense air moves towards the Equator (from the poles) and undercuts warm air to force it aloft. It is associated with a high chance of thunderstorms. While the front is passing, wind veers and pressure drops.

MET SERVICES

ATIS: met report available at certain airports on VHF, VOR and NDB frequencies. They are updated every 30 minutes or whenever a significant update occurs.

VOLMET: long readouts of met reports in sequence of certain airports

METAR: met reports of met conditions issued every 30 minutes. "TREND" or "NOSIG" words indicate a validity of 2 hrs of the conditions described.

TAF: met forecast of an aerodrome, between 9 to 24 hrs before. The first ones are updated every 3 h and the last ones every 6 h. "TEMPO" conditions within a TAF are expected to last less than 1 h.

SIGMET: warning of serious weather. Their normal life is 4 h.

In the next few pages you will find NOTAM, METAR and Significant Weather Chart decoders.

NOTAM DECODER

Descriptor	
MI	Shallow
PR	Partial
BC	Patches
BL	Blowing
SH	Showers
TS	Thunderstorms
FZ	Freezing
Precipitation	
DZ	Drizzle
RA	Rain
SN	Snow
SG	Snow Grains
IC	Ice Crystals
PL	Ice Pellets
GR	Hail
GS	Small Hail/Snow Pellets
UP	Unknown
Obscuration	
BR	Mist
FG	Fog

FU	Smoke
VA	Volcanic Ash
DU	Dust
SA	Sand
HZ	Haze
Other	
PO	Dust/Sand Whirls
SQ	Squalls
FC	Tornado/Watersprout
SS	Sandstorm
DS	Duststorm
WS	Windshear
Low visibility	
R	RVR
M	Below minima
P	More than assessed
D	Decreasing
U	Increasing
Clouds	
EMBD	Embedded
OCNL	Occasional

SIGNIFICANT WEATHER CHART DECODER

⟨symbol⟩	Thunderstorms	⟨symbol⟩	Drizzle
⟨symbol⟩	Tropical cyclone	⟨symbol⟩	Rain
⟨symbol⟩	Severe squall line	★	Snow
⟨symbol⟩	Moderate turbulence	▽	Shower
⟨symbol⟩	Severe turbulence	△	Hail
◯	Mountain waves	⟨symbol⟩	Widesprad blowing snow
⟨symbol⟩	Moderate aircraft icing	S	Severe sand or dust haze
⟨symbol⟩	Severe aircraft icing	⟨symbol⟩	Widespread sandstorm or duststorm
≡	Widespread fog	∞	Widespread haze
⟨symbol⟩	Radioactive materials in the atmosphere	=	Widespread mist
⟨symbol⟩	Volcanic eruption	⟨symbol⟩	Widespread smoke
⟨symbol⟩	Mountain obscuration	⟨symbol⟩	Freezing precipitation

▲▲	Cold front at the surface	⟨symbol⟩	State of the sea
⌒⌒	Warm front at the surface	⟨18⟩	Sea-surface temperature
▲⌒▲⌒	Occluded front at the surface	⟨0°:100⟩	Freezing level
⌒▼⌒▼	Quasi-stationary front at the surface	⟨40⟩	Widespread strong suface wind (> 30 kt)
15 →	Direction and speed (kt) of displacement	⟨symbol⟩	Convergence line

Source: aemet.es

SNOWTAM DECODER

The following table is a SNOWTAM decoder using the example below:

07/5/9/05/93 — RR/T/E/DD/BB

RR —Runway designator	
07	Runway affected
+50	Add 50 if parallel RWY to indicate "R" RWY.
88	Inf. applies to all RWY
99	Repetition of last report
T — Type of deposit	
0	Clear and dry
1	Damp
2	Wet or water patches
3	Rime (<1 mm deep)
4	Dry snow
5	Wet snow
6	Slush
7	Ice
8	Compact or rolled snow
9	Frozen ruts or ridges
/:	not notified
E — Extent of contamination	
1	Less than 10 %
2	Less than 25 %
5	Less than 50 %
9	50-100 %
/:	not notified

DD — Depth of deposit	
00	Less than 1 mm
01-90	Depth in mm
92	100 mm
93	150 mm
94	200 mm
95	250 mm
96	300 mm
97	350 mm
98	400 mm
99	RWY not operational
//	Depth not significant or measurable
BB — Braking conditions	
01-90	Friction coefficient
91	BA Poor
92	BA Medium-Poor
93	BA Medium
94	BA Medium-Good
95	BA Good
99	BA Unrealiable or not measurable
OTHERS	
CLRD	Contamination cleared
SNOCLO	Airport closed

4. BASICS — OTHER

COMMUNICATIONS, AIR LAW AND FLIGHT PLANNING

Loss of communications

According to ICAO —Annex 2—, a flight under IMC conditions or IFR rules losing two-way communication should maintain the last assigned speed and level (or minimum flight altitude if higher) for a minimum of 7 minutes following:

- Last assigned level or minimum altitude is reached, or
- The time the transponder is set to 7600, or
- The aircraft failure to report its position over a compulsory reporting point,

Whichever is later. Then adjust flight path according to the flight plan. Take the following into consideration:

- If being radar vectored, rejoin the flight plan at the next significant waypoint taking terrain into account.
- Proceed along your flight plan towards the navaid serving the destination airport.
- At the last acknowledged ETA, or as close as possible to the ETA resulting from your current flight plan, commence the descent.
- Land within 30 minutes of ETA or last acknowledged EAT, whichever is later.
- If all attempts to establish communications by other channels or in other frequencies fail, transmit each message twice preceded by the phrase "TRANSMITTING BLIND". PIC intentions should be communicated too.

Holding patterns

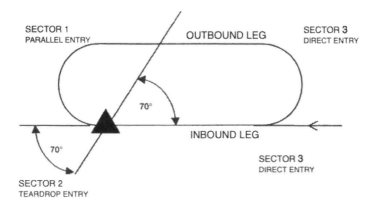

The outbound leg is timed at 1:00 below FL140, and 1:30 above FL140.

Holding patterns have a *buffer area* which extends 5 nm beyond the holding area.

Entry from *Sector 1* entails flying to the fix, fly parallel to the inbound leg for 1 minute (with wind corrections), and then a turn greater than 180º inside the holding area in order to intercept the inbound leg towards the fix (**Parallel** Entry).

Entry from *Sector 2* entails flying to the fix and then turn onto a heading which is 30 degrees offset the inbound track. Fly for 1 minute (with wind corrections) and then turn inbound (**Teardrop** entry)

Entry from *Sector 3* entails flying to the fix and commencing the holding directly from there (**Direct** entry). However, if the turn from the fix to the outbound leg is less than 180 degrees, some adjustments will have to be applied. If the turn is less than 180 degrees but greater than 70º, hold your heading for between 5 and 15 seconds before turning outbound.

Procedure turns

Explained in the following picture from ICAO:

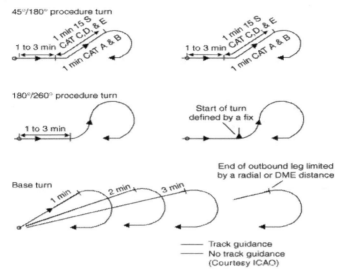

Area navigation

Area navigation is a method of IFR navigation that allows an aircraft to choose any course within a network of beacons rather than flying directly from or to one of the beacons. Area navigation used to be called "Random Navigation", hence the acronym R-NAV.

An R-NAV specification is designated as RNAV X, for instance, RNAV 1. The number specifies de required lateral accuracy in nautical miles, which is expected to be achieved, at least, 95 % of the time.

- **RNP** specifications include a requirement for on-board performance monitoring and alerting.
- **RNAV** specifications do NOT include a requirement for on-board performance monitoring and alerting.

RNP4, RNP2 AND RNAV 10 (Or RNP 10) are designed for oceanic and remote navigation applications.

RNP1, RNAV1, RNAV2, RNAV5 are designed for terminal areas.

RNP AR, RNP APCH and APCH are designated for approach areas (0.3 NM accuracy).

For RNP APP, the following must be taken into account:

RNAV (GNSS) Z 09L

RNP APCH GNSS required

- Direct to FAF is not permitted.
- Direct to before FAF only permitted if established at least 2 NM before FAF and intercepting angle <45º.
- Procedure cannot be modified in the FMGS.

Transition levels and altitudes

Cruising levels are expressed in terms of:

- Flight levels: based on 1013.25, or QNE. It is the altimeter reading with 2 digits knocked off from the end. FL300 is 30 000 ft.
- Altitudes: based on QNH, expressed in feet.
- Height: based on QFE, or airfield elevation.

The change-over from FL to altitudes is based on the following criteria:

- The Transition Altitude is the indicated altitude above which the standard setting must be selected by the crew.
- The Transition Level is the first available flight level above the transition altitude.

The change between the QNH setting and Standard setting occurs at the transition altitude when climbing, and at the transition level when descending (see the following table):

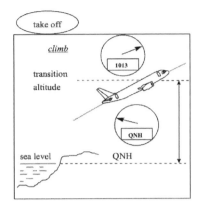
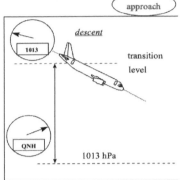

Altimetry

Aircraft pressure altimeters read the elevation of the A/C above a defined datum. If the pilot fails to set the correct datum (QNH or FL), then the results could be catastrophic.

For instance, if an A/C is authorized to descend to 4000 ft on QNH 993, but the pilots fail to set QNH and descend on STD (FL), then the A/C would fly 540 ft lower!

Real altitude is 4000 ft on QNH = 993.

If the pilots fly with a datum of 1013, then they are making the A/C believe that it is flying on a higher pressure environment, and therefore lower (remember, pressure decreases with altitude).

Minimum Safe Altitudes

- o **MSA**: in terminal area, 25 nm of a defined navaid.
- o **MEA** (Enroute): Airway Centerline, number on airway

- o **MOCA** (Enroute): 4nm either side of Airway Centerline, number with "T": 7000T.
- o **MORA** (Off-route): 10nm of airway centerline, number with "A" (6000A)

o <u>Grid</u> <u>MORA</u> (Off-route): within defined grid sector

Transponder codes

7500: Hijacking

7600: Communication failure

7700: Emergency onboard

2000: recognize A/C without transponder assigned

7000: VFR standard code

Marshalling signals

We have included a few marshalling signals, especially the ones that are not that common or evident, so that you can always have them in mind:

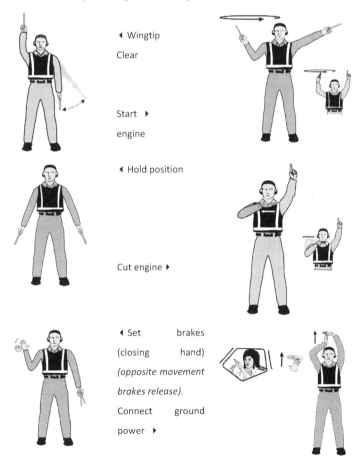

27

◀ Chocks inserted (released is opposite movement)

Fire ▶

Meteorological visibility to RVR

This procedure is not allowed in the following cases:

- Reported RVR is available
- Take-off minima calculation
- RVR minima less than 800 m

In case that the pilot wanted to convert from visibility to RVR, he or she should follow the following table:

Light elements	Day	Night
HI approach and RWY lights	1.5	2.0
Any type of lighting apart from the above	1.0	1.5
No lights	1.0	n/a

RVR achieved by a product of the known visibility times one of the factored numbers above.

ALTERNATE POLICY

Take-off alternate: shall be located within one hour flight time in single engine condition in still air. A take-off alternate is required when the departing airport is below the operator's established landing minima or when there are reasons to believe that an immediate return to the departure station would not be possible. The take-off alternate selection only has into account the current aircraft limitations (A/C status) and a possible engine failure during departure.

Destination alternate: at least <u>one destination</u> alternate should be selected unless:

1) There is certainty that the landing will be completed in VMC, and

Two separated and independent runways are available, and

At least one of them has a PA.

2) The airport is isolated, if a PNR is selected and 2 hrs worth of extra endurance are added as final reserve.

<u>Two destination</u> alternates must be selected if:

1) Meteorological conditions are below the operator's established minima*

2) There is no meteorological information.

The operator's established minima normally takes into account that airport conditions at the ETA plus or minus 1 h, which is broadly accepted in Europe as an acceptable timeframe.

Type of approach	Planning minima (Destination and Alt.)
CAT II and III	CAT I
CAT I	NPA
NPA	NPA +200m/+1000 ft
Circling	Circling

The application of aerodrome forecast (weather) is detailed in a table contained in ICAO Annex 3. A brief summary can be found below:

- Mean winds are taken into account and gusts may be disregarded.
- Any deterioration would count from the start of the change.
- Any improvement would count from the end of the change.
- TEMPO or PROB30/40 conditions that are transient (SH, TS...) may be disregarded.

- TEMPO or PROB30/40 conditions that are permanent (HZ, MI, FG...) are applicable.
- Any improvement with TEMPO or PROB 30/40 may be disregarded.
- PROB TEMPO may be disregarded.

WEIGHTS

In the following picture you will find a brief explanation of all weights used in aviation.

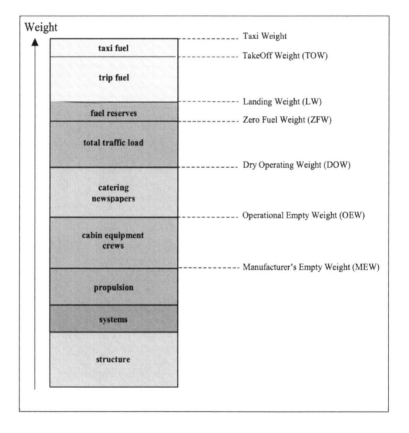

SEPARATION

Aircraft separation has to be achieved in different levels or areas:

Take-off and landing

normally takes into account wake turbulence. It is applied during landing, take-off, and during A/C movements near the airfield with aircrafts with a minimum vertical separation of 1000 ft, or where concern about wake turbulence separation exists.

Landing separation:

Leading A/C	Following A/C	Separation (nm)	Separation (min)
Heavy	Heavy	4	
Heavy	**Medium**	5	2
Heavy	Light	6	3
Medium	Heavy	3	
Medium	**Medium**	3	
Medium	Light	5	3
Light	Heavy	3	
Light	**Medium**	3	
Light	Light	3	

Departure separation:

It is way easier as it could be basically summarized as follows: **2 min** is the standard timing between departures, increasing to **3 min** if following A/C is departing from an intermediate portion of the runway.

Vertical separation

is achieved by operating at different flight levels. RVSM is used between FL290 and FL410 in order to reduce vertical separation from 2000 to 1000 ft.

Parallel runways

Parallel runways are used to increase capacity. In order for them to function independently they must be separated by at least 610 m.

Longitudinal separation

A/C on the same track normally have a separation of 15 minutes, which can be reduced to 10 minutes where navigation aids permit frequent determination of position and speed. Additionally, separation may be reduced to 5 minutes if the leading A/C is at least 20 kts faster, or 3 min if it is at least 40 kts faster.

DME distances may also be used, in which case distance is 20 nm, or 10 nm if the lead A/C is at least 20 kts faster.

Airport signals

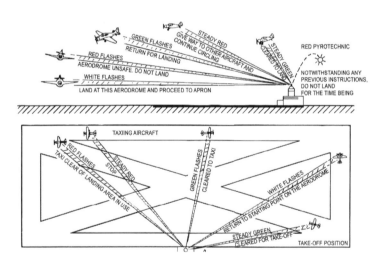

Interception signals

Interception signals from military A/C are described below:

Intercepting A/C	Meaning	Intercepted A/C	Meaning
Rocking A/C and flashing NAV lights	You have been intercepted, follow me	Rocking A/C and flashing NAV lights	I will comply
Abrupt breakaway consisting in a turning turn of at least 90º.	You may proceed	Rocking the A/C	Understood
Lowering landing gear, steady landing lights and overflying the RWY	Land at this airport	Lower landing gear, steady landing lights and follow the intercepting A/C.	Understood, I will comply
Intercepted A/C	**Meaning**	**Intercepting A/C**	**Meaning**
Regular flashing of all lights	I am in distress		
Regular switching ON and OFF of all available lights, but not in a flashing manner.	Cannot comply		

Adherence to flight plans

Aircrafts should adhere to their active flight plan and communicate to ATC any deviations which result in a change of speed of 5 % or more, or a change in the ETA/ETA for the next waypoint of plus or minus 3 minutes.

HUMAN FACTORS

Hypoxia

Hypoxia is a condition where oxygen concentration in the blood is below normal, or where oxygen cannot be used by the body.

Symptoms include:

- o   Personality and judgement changes
- o   Muscle movement sluggish
- o   Short-term memory loss
- o   Loss of consciousness
- o   Blueness/Cyanosis

Hypoxia is treated by increasing the individual's oxygen supply.

Hyperventilation

is the condition of over breathing caused by an excess of oxygen. Might be caused by hypoxia, as well as by anxiety, heat or motion sickness for instance.

Symptoms are:

- o   Dizziness
- o   Tingling sensation
- o   Hot or cold feelings
- o   Anxiety
- o   Reduced performance
- o   Loss of consciousness

Hyperventilation is normally treated by making the individual breathe into a paper bag. However, due to its symptoms being very close to hypoxia, it is recommended to treat these symptoms as hypoxia if the aircraft is above 10 000 ft.

Carbon monoxide

Carbon monoxide is produced by fuel combustion. Its particles can attach themselves to humans' hemoglobin, starving the brain and body of oxygen. Symptoms are:

- o Cherry red skin
- o Headache, dizziness or nausea
- o Impaired judgement
- o Slower breathing rate
- o Loss of consciousness

Illusions

Very common in aviation. Described below:

Problem	Illusion	Risk
Downslope	Too low	High approach
Upslope	Too high	Low approach
Rain	Closer	Low approach
Narrow	Too high	Low approach
Wide	Too low	High approach and flare
Bright lights	Too low	High approach
Kraft illusion or black hole	Too high, due to the illusion of nothing moving while continuing the approach	Low approach

5.   A320   —   LIMITATIONS, PERFORMANCE AND MEL

Dimensions (a320)	Length ....37.57 m
	Width ....34.1 m
	Height ....12.14 m
General	Load acceleration limits
	o Clean configuration............................. -1g to +2.5g
	o Other configurations................................ 0g to +2g
	Runway slope... +/- 2%
	Runway altitude .... 9 200 ft
	Nominal/Minima runway width 45m/30m
	Max operating altitude .... 39 800 ft
Speeds	MMO.. 0.82
	VMO.. 350 kt
	VLE .... 280 kt / M = 0.67
	VLO$_{ext}$ .... 250 kt / M = 0.60
	VLO$_{ret}$ .... 220 kt / M = 0.54
	F:1 .... 230 kt
	F:1+F .... 215 kt
	F:2 .... 200 kt
	F:3 ....185 kt
	F: FULL .... 177 kt

	Wipers maximum ....230 kt
	Auto flap retraction ....210 kt
	Cockpit window open ....200 kt
	Max tire speed ....195 kt

	Vx .... Green dot

Vy ....260/M.76 (280 for A321)

Turbulence Penetration Speeds (<FL200/>200/>320)

CFM.. 250/275/M0.76

LEAP1A 260/280/M0.76

Pressure

Max positive differential pressure ....9.0 PSI

Max negative differential pressure.................................. -1.0 PSI

Ram air max difference..1 PSI

Safety relief valve setting...8.6 PSI

Max Normal Cabin Altitude .... 8000 ft

Min Normal Cabin Altitude... 2000ft

Cabin Altitude Warning .... 9550 ft

Max Cabin Altitude Selection.. 14 000 ft

Autopilot

Take off .... 100 ft AGL and at least 5s after lift off

Disconnection

PA ....80 % of minima

NPA .... MDA/DA

Visual .... 500 ft

Circling .... minima -100 ft

Fuel

Minimum fuel temperature...-43ºC

Maximum fuel temperature 54ºC

Minimum fuel at T/O 1500kg

RVSM

Ground, PFD vs Airport .... 75 ft

Ground, PFD1 vs PFD2 .... 20 ft

Ground, PFD vs ISIS (digital/mech) ....60/300 ft

In flight...SEE FCOM PRO-SPO-50

180º turn

min RWY

width

A319... 31.1 m

A320... 28.7 m

A321... 33.1 m

Slats&Flaps

Max Extended .... 20 000 ft

Wind

Passenger door ....65 kt

	Cargo door ....40 kt
	Max X-wind 320 ....38 kt
	Max X-wind 320$_{neo}$ ....35 kt
Engine	TOGA (all ENG/SE) .... 5 min/10 min
and APU	Oil Temp (MAX/MIN/TO MIN) ....140/-40/50 ºC
	ENG Start/............. 4 attempts with 20s pause, 15m cooling after
	APU start.................................... 3 attempts, 60m wait after that.
	CFM min oil:.. 9.5 qts + 0.5/h
	IAE min oil: .... 11 qts + 0.3/h
	P&W min oiL ....14 qts
	NOTE: check your company policy
Gen&	APU Generator.. 39 000 ft
Bleed	APU start on BAT .... 25 000 ft
Limits	1 pack ,... 22 500 ft
	Engine start.. 20 000 ft
	2 packs .... 15 000 ft
A/C striking	Pitch (A318/A319/A320/A321)
the ground	Strut compressed:.................................. 15.7º/13.9º/11.7º/9.7º
	Strut extended 17.3º/15.5º/13.5º/11.2º
	Bank 16º

PERFORMANCE FACTS

The following facts are A320 performance specific issues that might come handy in your day to day operations. This information is additional to the one already given in section 4.

A320 facts:

- MAX TOGA time is 5 minutes for all engines operative and 10 minutes for OEI.
- One engine taxi out savings are around 40 kg per event.
- APU uses around 160kg/h.

- The flexible temperature is the input parameter that adapts the A/C the thrust to the actual take off weight.
- Thrust reduction cannot exceed 25 % of the maximum available thrust.
- FLEX take off increases fuel consumption by less than 5 kg.
- FLEX T/O is allowed on wet runways but not on contaminated runways.
- TOGA is always available on T/O even if FLX is selected first.
- The actual OEI climb performance is diminished by 1,1 % in comparison with the all engines climb performance.
- Most efficient climb in the A320 is obtained using Mach 0.76/280 kts. Increasing speed from 280 to 330 kts decreases time by 6 % but increases fuel burn by 6 % too. In absolute values, 90 seconds are saved but around 80 kg more are used.
- Contrary to what happens with other aircrafts and with the rest of the Airbus family, CG position does not have a significant effect on the fuel consumption.
- Flying 4000 ft below the optimum altitude has an impact of around 5 % penalty on trip fuel, increasing to 10 % flying 6000 ft below it (up to 15 % in the A321).
- OPT FL in the FMGC gives a 0.3g buffet margin and rate of climb of 300 ft/min. Typical cruise distances between 2000 ft steps, in the A320, are around 1200 nm.
- Airbus philosophy assumes a minimum of 5 min leveled flight in the cruise.
- The increase of 1000 kg above planned fuel gives an approximate 50 kg penalty of fuel for every 1000 nm (A321, less for other variants).
- Green dot speed is the best speed for economy descent and for holding.
- The difference in fuel burn between a 240 kt descent and a 300 kt descent is around 50kg, saving around 150 seconds.
- Fuel consumption at low level is around 5 kg/nm.
- Fuel for "alternate" includes 100kg for G/A, climb fuel, trip and descend fuel calculations to the alternate airport.

Flex temperature philosophy

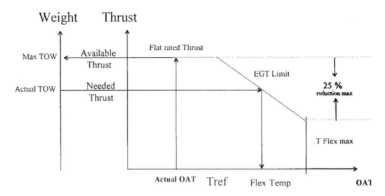

note: the 25% of maximum reduction is a requirement that allows the A/C the quickly regain max power if needed.

Cost Index vs Fuel and Time in the A320

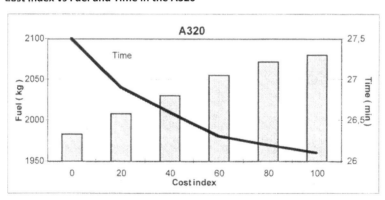

Minimum Control Speeds

Altitude	VMCA	VMCG (KT IAS)		
(ft)	(KT CAS)	CONF 1 + F	CONF 2	CONF 3
0	110	109.5	107.5	107
2000	108	107.5	105.5	105
4000	107.5	107	105	104.5
6000	105.5	105	103	102.5
8000	103	102.5	100.5	100
9200	101.2	100.5	98.5	98

40

STALLING SPEEDS

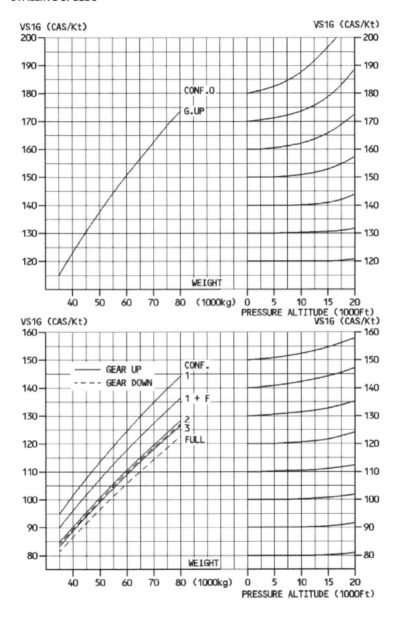

LIMITATIONS

When calculating your take off distance in the EFB, the process results in two limitation codes from the table below:

TOW	Take off Weight	TIRE	tyre speed
RWY0	Limited by TOD 2 ENG	2SEG	2nd segment performance
RWY1	Limited by TOD SE	VMU	Minimum Unstick Speed
VMCG	Minimum control speed grou	OBS	Obstacles
BRK	Brake Energy		

MEL and MMEL

The *minimum equipment list (MEL)* is a document that allows airlines to operate with some equipment unserviceable for a limited time. MELs are a list of items and equipment installed on an aircraft, showing how many of them can be defective and for how long.

MELs are based on the *master minimum equipment list (MMEL)*, which is produced by the manufacturer. Then every airline adapts the document to their own needs. However, MEL cannot be less restrictive than the original MMEL.

The MMEL/MEL is applicable up to the commencement of the flight (i.e., the point in which the aircraft starts to move under its own power in preparation for take off).

All MEL entries can be classified as:

"GO" — A/C is dispatchable

"GO IF" —A/C is dispatchable within the specified rectification interval, but only if an operational procedure by the crew (o) or/and a maintenance procedure (m) is performed.

"NO GO" —A/C is not dispatchable.

Rectification intervals

The MMEL establishes limitations on the amount of time that an A/C can fly with inoperative items.

Rectification intervals:	A	B	C	D
Consecutive Calendar Days:	Refer to dispatch conditions	3 days	10 days	120 days

These intervals may be extended once, twice in some countries depending on local regulations.

Maintenance messages

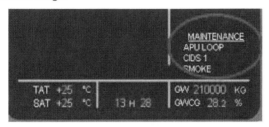

Maintenance messages only appear on the ground after engine shutdown and before engine start-up. All maintenance status messages on the A320 are "GO" and classified with a rectification interval "C" or "D", except for the following ones:

BLUE RSVR — NO GO // AIR BLEED — GO IF

Each maintenance message is displayed at the beginning of its relevant chapter in the MEL.

Multiple unserviceabilities

As stated in ACJ MMEL/MEL.030, the MMEL does not consider all combinations of unserviceabilities: "It has to be accepted that because of the variety of multiple unserviceabilities which could arise, it is likely that many will not be covered in the MMEL".

Therefore, if several pieces of equipment are inoperative, Operators should consult the MEL for each item, to check if there are any incompatibilities between all associated dispatch conditions. It is the flight crew's responsibility to assess the situation and to decide whether or not to accept multiple unserviceabilities.

6. PNEUMATIC — 36

The **pneumatic air** provides high-pressure air for:

- Air conditioning
- Engine starting
- Wing anti-icing
- Water pressurization
- Hydraulic reservoir pressurization
- FWD Cargo heating
- AFT Cargo heating
- Fuel Tank Inerting System (FTIS)

The pneumatic power has three different sources: Engine bleed systems, APU load compressor and HP ground connection. APU bleed has **priority** over ENG bleed.

Engine bleed is provided through two Engine bleed valves, which close automatically when the following is detected:

- APU bleed valve open
- Engine Start
- Over temperature
- Leak
- Over Pressure

The vale is also closed pneumatically when low pressure or reverse flow ins detected, or electrically when either the ENG BLEED P/B is selected OFF, or when the ENG FIRE P/B is selected.

Let's see the schematics:

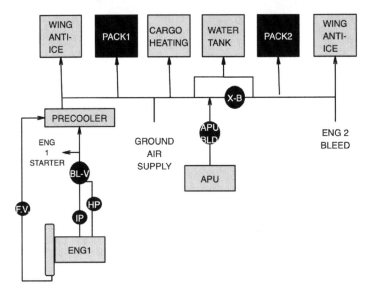

BL-V: *Engine Bleed Valve*
IP: *Intermediate Pressure Stage*
HP: *High Pressure Stage*
F.V.:*Fan Air Valve*
X-B: *Cross-bleed valve*

Two Bleed Monitoring Computers (**BMC**) control and monitor the operation of the pneumatic system. If one BMC fails, the other one takes over most of its functions. Normally BMC1 controls the left side engine and APU bleed, whereas BMC2 controls the rest.

Air is normally bled from the IP stage of the engine's HP compressor. At low engine speed, when the pressure and the temperature of the IP are too low, air is bled from the HP and maintains a pressure around 36 PSI (around 65 for A320$_{neo}$).

PNEUMATIC — INDICATIONS AND ECAM

PNEUMATIC — ECAM

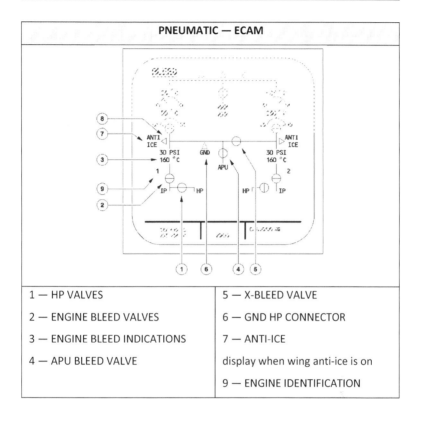

1 — HP VALVES	5 — X-BLEED VALVE
2 — ENGINE BLEED VALVES	6 — GND HP CONNECTOR
3 — ENGINE BLEED INDICATIONS	7 — ANTI-ICE
4 — APU BLEED VALVE	display when wing anti-ice is on
	9 — ENGINE IDENTIFICATION

PNEUMATIC — ABNORMAL

AIR - ENG 1(2) BLEED HI TEMP	If wing anti-ice OFF, turn off affected side pack, If wing anti-ice ON, turn off wing anti-ice first.
AIR - ENG 1(2) BLEED LO TEMP	Disconnect A/THR Increase affected ENG Thrust
AIR - ENG 1(2) BLEED FAULT	Turn off affected side engine bleed. If wing anti-ice OFF, PACK FLOW to LO Open X-bleed valve
AIR ENG 1(2) BLEED NOT CLOSED	this warning might be triggered due to residual pressure between the HP or IP valves and the engine bleed valve after engine shut down or APU BLEED selected OFF. Procedure requests to shut the ENG BLEED affected OFF.
AIR ENG 1(2) BLEED LEAK	The alert triggers when both pylon bleed leak detection loops detected a temperature above 204ºC. The procedure asks to shut the ENG BLEED off, X BLEED shut and wing anti-ice off.
AIR - ENG 1+2 BLEED FAULT	RESET offered first by ECAM or QRH If unsuccessful, rapid descent is initiated. If APU is started and BLEED available, PRESS is recovered and MAX FL200 is recommended When at or below FL100, RAM AIR is opened when CAB PR >1 psi.
AIR - PACK 1(2) OVHT	This alert triggers when: • The pack compressor outlet temperature rises above 260ºC • The pack compressor outlet temperature rises above 230ºC four times during the same flight.

	• The pack outlet temperature rises above 95ºC The procedure asks to turn the affected pack OFF, which might be recovered if the overheat conditions disappears.
AIR - PACK 1(2) REGUL FAULT	This alert triggers when: • The temperature regulation performance is degraded (crew awareness only) • An inconsistency is detected between air flow taken on the engine computed by the EIU and pack flow computed by ACSC (pack lost on the ground)

7. AIR CONDITIONING, PRESSURIZATION AND VENTILATION — 21

AIR CONDITIONING

Air is supplied via:

- Two pack flow control valves

- Two packs

- The mixing unit, which mixes the air that comes from the cabin and the packs.

The **air conditioning** system is fully automatic and provides continuous air renewal, maintaining constant temperature in three zones: COCKPIT, FWD CABIN AND AFT CABIN.

Aircraft temperature can be controlled by the cockpit's AIR COND panel. Temperature regulation of the temperature is ensured by:

- One zone controller and two pack controllers,

- Or by two Air Conditioning System Controller (ACSC)

Temperature control is optimized via the hot air pressure regulating valve.

Let's see a schematics in the following page:

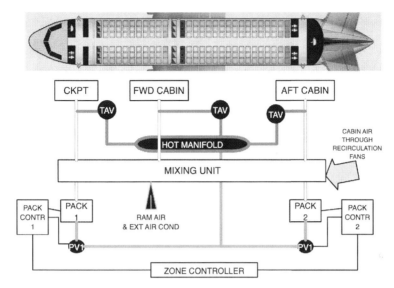

TAV: Trim-Air Valve

Pack Flow control valves regulate the air flow in accordance with commands from the two pack controllers.

The Flight Crew uses the temperature selectors on the overhead panel to select the desired temperature. The actual temperature is measured in the Cockpit, In the lavatory extraction circuit and in the galley ventilation system.

A temperature control panel is also available in the FAP. The Cabin Crew may modify the cockpit selected temperature by plus or minus 2,5ºC.

The lowest demanded temperature is sent to the packs. The warmer ones are modified through the Trim Air Valves.

PACK CONTROLLER FAILURES

Each pack controller has two channels, known as the primary and the secondary channel.

- If the primary channel fails, the other one takes over.
- If the secondary channel fails, the primary takes over with no effect on temperature optimization, but ECAM signals are lost.

 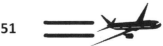

- If both controllers fail, the pack outlet temperature is controlled by the pack anti-ice valve to a temperature between 5 and 30º C in a maximum of 6 minutes. ECAM signals corresponding to that pack are lost.

ZONE CONTROLLER FAILURES

Each zone controller has two channels, known as the primary and secondary channels.

- If the primary channel fails, the secondary takes over and: hot air and trim air valves close, zones are controlled at 24ºC, pack one controls the CKCPT temperature, and pack two FWD and AFTR cabin temperatures. ALTN MODE appears on ECAM.
- If the secondary channel fails, there is no effect on zone temperature regulation.
- If both channels fail, packs deliver a fixed temperature: 20º C for pack 1 and 10º C for pack 2. All ECAM COND ECAM page is lost and the message PACK REG is displayed.

PRESSURIZATION

The pressurization system is made up of two identical automatic systems called CPC (Cabin Pressure Controllers), plus:

- One outflow valve with three electric motors, one for manual control
- Two safety valves, which prevent cabin pressure from exceeding 8,6 psi or going below 1 psi below ambient pressure.
- One control panel

Normally one CPC controls the whole system while the other one is on standby. A changeover occurs 70 s after landing or when one of the two systems fail.

The automatic sequence works as follows:

- <u>Ground:</u> before T/O and 55s after landing, the Outflow valve fully opens to ensure that there is no residual cabin pressure.

- <u>Take-off</u>: When THR LEVERS are advanced, the cabin is pre-pressurized at a rate of 400 ft/min until ΔP reaches 0.1 psi.

- <u>Climb</u>: Cabin altitude varies according to the fixed pre-programmed law, which depends on the actual rate of climb.

- <u>Cruise</u>: Cabin altitude is maintained.

- <u>Descent</u>: Cabin altitude descends to equal the landing field pressure with a maximum rate of 750 ft/min.

Depressurization

Depressurization may occur due to system malfunction or damage to the aircraft causing a breach in the aircraft structure.

Rapid depressurization is indicated by:

- Drop in temperature

- Fog appearance due to condensation

- Loud noise

- Suction of objects

The major risk is the lack of oxygen and the TUC. Remember, TUC at 35 000 ft between 30 and 60s.

Remember, masks drop automatically when the cabin pressure exceeds 14 000 ft.

KNOW YOUR FACTS...

- If the pilot suspects that pressurization is not performing normally but the system has not failed yet, press the MODE SEL PB to MAN for 10 secs. This will cause the systems to swap.

Emergency descent

Should be performed in case of:

- Rapid or Explosive Depressurization
- Excessive or uncontrollable cabin altitude or V/S

However, the cabin crew must rely on the **CAB PR EXCESS CAB ALT** warning even if not confirmed on the CAB PRESS SD.

The emergency procedure is normally a two-step procedure as follows:

- First: memory items (as indicated in section 18).
- Second: Perform the read&do procedure (ECAM or QRH). Consider TCAS Below for better traffic awareness and remember that some countries CRAR might have different procedures (for instance, HDG in the UK is maintained when performing an emergency descent).

A **MAYDAY** call should be done:

"MAYDAY, MAYDAY, MAYDAY, Monarch 302W, Emergency descent"

Rapid descent

Should be performed in case of slow depressurization (Cabin V/S < 1000 ft / min). However, take into account that slow pressurizations can quickly get worse and a swift descent is recommended in all cases.

It can be caused by:

- System failure: BLEED, PACK, Pressure control systems...
- Aircraft slight damage, including window cracking or impaired sealings.

Slow depressurization is indicated by:

- Abnormal cabin altitude or V/S
- Abnormal noises
- Ear pain, headache or any incapacitation

Crew should don their oxygen masks whenever the cabin altitude is above 10.000 ft or any symptoms of hypoxia are felt.

PAX oxygen masks should be dropped when cabin altitude is at or above 14.000 ft, as the main objective of a rapid descent is to avoid that from happening.

A rapid descent is a normal descent that is trying to avoid pax oxygen masks deploying. So we have to take into consideration:

- The current cabin altitude.
- The difference between our current altitude and a safe altitude, normally between FL100 and FL140 (or higher, taking into account terrain considerations).

So for instance, if we are flying at FL310 (which is our maximum with a single BLEED fault, which might lead to a DUAL BLEED FAULT and therefore to a slow decompression) with a cabin altitude of 6000 ft and would like to descent to FL100, we would have to calculate:

1) Altitude loss: 21 000 ft

2) Time available at maximum loss of V/S (1000 ft, as more than that is considered an emergency descent): difference between 6000 ft and 14 000 ft: 8000 ft, which translates as 8 min.

3) We divide the altitude loss by time, and we have an average rate of descent of around 2 700 ft/min.

HOWEVER, take into account that the air loss might become higher.

VENTILATION

Avionics

The avionics are cooled through a system that uses two openings and two electric fans. Conditioned air is also available as a backup if needed.

See the schematics in the following page. The table below it specifies which valves and fans are open or close for every configuration:

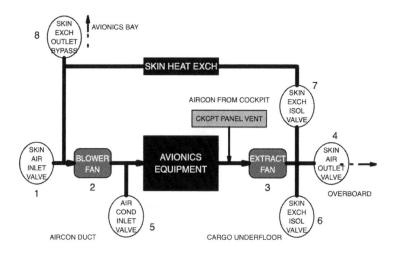

Open? ==>	Open Config	Closed config	Intermediate	Abnormal - Blower override	Abnormal - Extract override	Smoke configuration
1.Skin Air Inlet Valve	✔	✘	✘	✘	✘	✘
2.Blower Fan	✔	✔	✔	✘	✔	✘
3.Extract Fan	✔	✔	✔	✔	✔	✔
4.Skin Air Outlet Valve	✔	✘	Int	✘	✘	Int
5.Air Conditioning Inlet Valve	✘	✘	✘	✔	✔	✔
6.Skin Exchange	✘	✔	✔	✘	✘	✘
7.Skin Exchange Isolation Valve	✘	✔	✔	✔	✔	✘
8. Skin Exchange Outlet By-pass valve	✘	✔	✔	✘	✘	✘

✔ = open, ✘ = closed, int = intermediate position

<u>Open</u> circuit configuration: when the A/C is on the ground and the skin temperature is above 12º C and increasing.

<u>Close</u> circuit configuration: when the A/C is on the ground with skin temperature of 9º C and decreasing, or inflight if the skin temperature is below 32º C and decreasing.

<u>Intermediate</u> configuration: inflight when skin temperature is above 35º C and increasing.

<u>Smoke</u> configuration: Blower and Extract buttons are set to override. The air conditioning system supplies cooling air which is then extracted overboard.

Lavatory and galley

A venture in the skin of the A/C draws air from both places and exhausts it overboard.

Cargo ventilation

Cargo compartments are ventilated with cabin air. An extraction fan draws air from the cargo compartment and exhausts it overboard.

AIR COND/PRESS/VENT — INDICATIONS AND ECAM

AIR CONDITIONING PANEL — CONTROLS

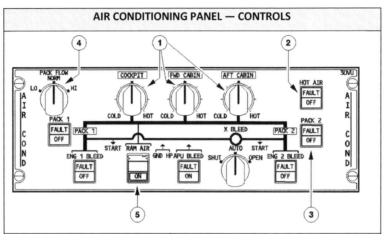

<u>1 — Zone temperature selector</u>	<u>4 — PACK FLOW sel</u>
12 o'clock position: 24ºC	◉ LO (80%)
COLD position: 18ºC	◉ NORM (100%)
HOT position 30ºC	◉ HI (120%)
<u>2 — HOT AIR P/B</u>	In case of single pack operation or APU
FAULT: overheat is detected (T	bleed supply, HI is automatically selected.
above 88ºC). Goes off if	Even if LO is selected, NORM is delivered
overheat condition disappears.	if demand cannot be satisfied.
<u>3 — PACK P/B</u>	<u>5 — RAM AIR (guarded)</u>
FAULT: Pack flow position	
disagrees with the selected	
position, or in case of overheat.	

AIR CONDITIONING PANEL — ECAM

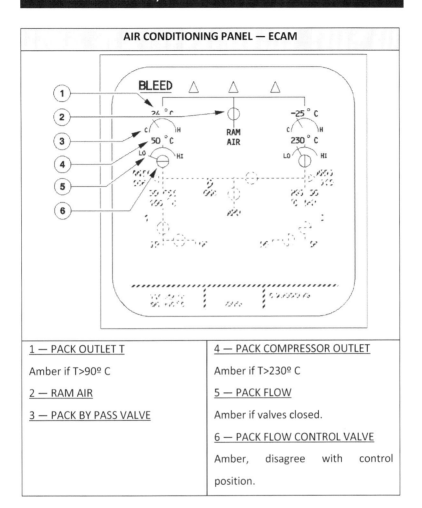

1 — PACK OUTLET T	4 — PACK COMPRESSOR OUTLET
Amber if T>90º C	Amber if T>230º C
2 — RAM AIR	5 — PACK FLOW
3 — PACK BY PASS VALVE	Amber if valves closed.
	6 — PACK FLOW CONTROL VALVE
	Amber, disagree with control position.

CABIN PRESS — PANEL

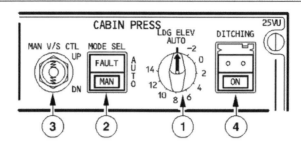

1 — LDG ELEV sel	3 — MAN V/S CTL
AUTO: FMGS optimization	Controls the outflow valve when (2) is in
Other: landing elevation is	MAN operation.
inserted manually. Refer to	UP: valve moves to the open position
ECAM for accurate selection.	DN: valve moves to the closed pos.
2 — MODE SEL PB	**4 — DITCHING P/B**
FAULT: both systems faulty	Outflow valve, ram air inlet, ventilation
	and pack flow control valves are closed.

TOP TIP!

The outflow valve operates slowly, so the pilot must hold the toggle switch in the UP or DN position until reaching the target V/S. CAUTION: there is a bit of a delay between switch manipulation and system response.

CABIN PRESS — ECAM

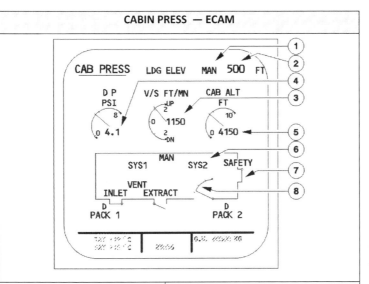

1 — LDG ELEV AUTO/MAN	5 — CABIN ALTITUDE
"AUTO" or "MAN".	Pulses if cabin is above 8800 ft.
2 — LDG ELEV	Red if Cabin < 9550 FT.
Altitude inserted manually or by the FMGS	6 — ACTIVE SYSTEM
	Green if active, amber if faulty.
3 — CABIN V/S	7 — SAFETY VALVE
Amber when V/S > 2000 ft/min	
4 — CABIN DIFF PRESS	
Amber if ΔP is less than 0.4 psi or more than 8.5 psi.	

AIR COND/PRESS/VENT — ABNORMAL

AIR - PACK1+2 FAULT	Turn off both packs Descend to higher of: FL100 or MEA *NOTE: if only one pack was overheated, reset possible when the overheating condition is out.*
CAB PR - SYS 1+2 FAULT	Manual pressurization mode. Guidance given by ECAM as shown in the picture.
CAB PR - SAFETY VALVE OPEN	If cabin differential <0 PSI, expect HI CAB RATE If cabin differential >8 PSI, use manual press. mode
CAB PR - CABIN OVER-PRESSURE	REFER TO QRH PROCEDURE, NO ECAM

	- with packs OFF and BLOWER and EXTRACT to OVRD, the cabin air is extracted overboard.
<u>CAB PR</u> - EXCESS CAB ALT	Triggering conditions: - 9550 ft cabin pressure. - 1000 ft above airfield pressure altitude. Requires an immediate rapid/emergency descent.
<u>COND</u> - HOT AIR FAULT	Turn off hot air. If unsuccessful, turn **both** packs OFF.
<u>VENT</u>- SKIN VALVE FAULT	Blower and Extract to OVRD If unsuccessful, descend to higher of FL100 or MEA.
<u>VENT</u> - AVNCS SYS FAULT	This alert triggers when: - Power up test not satisfactory - AEVC not supplied - Valve position disagrees with commanded position AVNCS VENT, BLOWER AND EXTRACT are INOP.

8. AUTOFLIGHT —22—

FMGS

The Flight Management Guidance System (FMGS) contains the following units:

- Two Flight Management Guidance Computers (FMGC). It contains a navigation database which is updated every 28 days, an airline modifiable information (AMI) with airline policy values and a performance database amongst others.
- Two Multipurpose Control and Display Units (MCDU) that allow data loading by the flight crew.
- One Flight Control Unit (FCU)
- Two Flight Augmentation Computers (FAC).

Each FMGS has four mode of operations:

- Dual mode: normal mode, the two FMGCs are synchronized.
- Independent mode: Both FMGCs working but not synchronized, in most cases because they have different databases. The message "INDEPENDENT OPERATION" will appear.
- Single mode: When one FMGC fails, both MCDUs are connected to the remaining FMGC. NDs must be set to the same range, otherwise the messages "MAP NOT AVAIL" and "SET OFFSIDE RNG/MODE" will appear.
- Back-up navigation: If both FMGCs fail some navigation function can be retrieved, mostly aircraft position, F-PLAN on ND, F-PLAN sequencing and limited lateral revisions.

The **autopilot (AP)** is normally linked to the FMGC is in use. When both autopilot are engaged (ILS approach), then FMGC1 is master.

NOTE: FMGS is an Airbus technicality, commonly known as FMS and also referred to using that acronym in various Airbus documents.

FCU

The Flight Control Unit (FCU) is the short-term interface between the flight crew and the FMGC and modifies the data inserted in the MCDU.

- ○ When a knob is pushed, managed modes are engaged.
- ○ When a knob is pulled, selected modes are engaged.

FAC

The Flight Augmentation computer controls the following functions:

- Controls rudder, rudder trim and yaw damper inputs.
- Computes data for the flight data envelope and speed functions.
- Provides warning for low-energy and windshear detection.

The windshear detection function is available:

- ○ At take-off, 3 s after lift off, up to 1 300 ft RA
- ○ At landing, from 1 300 ft RA to 50 ft RA
- ○ With at least CONF1 selected.

FD

The Flight Director (FD) displays guidance commands from the FMGC on the PFD. FD1 displays FMGC1 orders and FD2 displays FMGC2 orders. If one FD fails, both PFDs display the remaining FD (2FD2 in the FMGC, for instance).

If the Pitch FD Bar, or the Roll FD Bar **flash** permanently, it means that GLIDE data (in the first case) or LOC data (second) has been interrupted. The flash for 10s when there has been a reversion in the lateral profile (horizontal bar, reversion to HDG) or in the vertical profile (vertical bar, reversion to V/S).

Flight directors disappear when bank goes beyond 45º (comes back at 40º) and when pitch exceeds 25º UP or 13º DN.

FMA

The Flight Mode Annunciator (FMA), which is above the PFDs, shows the status of the A/THR, AP, FD and approach capabilities. A white box is displayed for 15 s around each new annunciation, increasing to 15s in case of reversion cases taking place, associated with a triple click. It has got three lines and five columns.

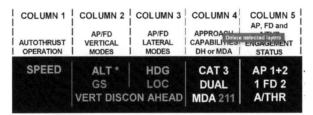

COLUMN 1	COLUMN 2	COLUMN 3	COLUMN 4	COLUMN 5
AUTOTHRUST OPERATION	AP/FD VERTICAL MODES	AP/FD LATERAL MODES	APPROACH CAPABILITIES DH or MDA	AP, FD and ENGAGEMENT STATUS
SPEED	ALT *	HDG	CAT 3	AP 1+2
	GS	LOC	DUAL	1 FD 2
	VERT DISCON AHEAD		MDA 211	A/THR

A/THR

The Autothrust is a function of the FMGS and includes two independent A/THR commands, one per each FMGC. They are able to control engine thrust by the Engine Control Units (ECU) in CFM Engines, and by the Electronic Engine Controls (EEC) in IAE Engines.

A/THR is armed by:

- Pushing A/THR PB on the FCU
- Setting THR Levers to FLX or TOGA with engines running on the ground
- Engaging the G/A mode.

A/THR is activated when, being armed:

- Two engines: thrust levers are set between CL and IDLE detents.
- Single engine: thrust levers are set between MCT and IDLE detents.

TOP TIP!

Ensure that you move the THR levers to match the current power setting before you disconnect the A/THR. If the A/THR is disconnected without moving the THR levers, current PWR setting will be commanded by the A/THR.

In all cases, the maximum A/THR thrust is set at the current thrust lever position. Remember that there are 6 THR Lever positions:

- ○ MAX REV
- ○ IDLE REV
- ○ IDLE
- ○ CL *(max climb)*
- ○ FLX (flex take off) and MCT (Max continuous thrust) detent.
- ○ TOGA

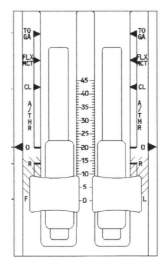

Manual thrust has a range between IDLE and CL in normal operation and between IDLE and MCT in single engine operations.

The **"THR LK"** message flashes in amber in the FMA when the thrust lock function is activated. It activates either when the A/THR is disconnected from the FCU (it should be disconnected from the instinctive P/B in the THR levers) or when there is a failure. Thrust is locked at previous level before disconnection.

CAUTION	If the flight crew pushes and holds the instinctive disconnect PB for more than 15s, the A/THR is disconnected for the remainder of the flight.

Alpha Floor

This protection is available from lift off to 100 ft RA in LDG configuration. It automatically sets the thrust at TOFA when the A/C reaches a very high angle of attack. The signal triggering Alpha Floor is generated via the FAC.

Alpha floor is inhibited when M>0.6 or when TCAS is engaged.

GS mini

The GS mini is an A/THR function that takes advantage of the aircraft inertia when the wind varies with the approach. The computation of the managed

speed target uses the tower headwind component (as inserted in the FMGC), the current headwind component and the Vapp.

So the managed speed target during the approach is calculated with the following formula:

$$\text{Managed speed} = \text{Vapp} + (\text{current HW} - \text{tower HW})$$

setting VFE-5 kt as a maximum speed in CONF FULL (VFE in all other flap configurations) and Vapp as a minimum speed.

A320 CHARACTERISTIC SPEEDS

Characteristic speeds are computed by the FAC according to the FMS weight data and aerodynamic data as a backup.

VS: stalling speed, is not displayed but serves as a base for all other speed computations. **VS1g** is the speed that can be demonstrated by flight tests. NOTE: authorities have agreed that a factor of 0.94 represents the relationship VS1g for aircraft of the A320 family and VSmin for conventional aircraft types.

VLS: Lowest Selectable Speed, computed by the FAC. Corresponds to:

- o   1.13 VS during take off or after a G/A
- o   1.23 VS after retraction of one step of flaps
- o   1.28 VS in clean configuration

F Speed: Minimum Speed at which flaps may be retracted at take off. Used as target speed for CONF2 and CONF3. Equals to about 1.23 VS of CONF1+F.

S Speed: Minimum speed at which the slats may be retracted on take off. In approach, used as target speed when in CONF1. Equal to about 1.29 VS of CLEAN CONFIG.

O (Green Dot): engine-out operating speed in clean config, best lift-to-drag ratio. Below 20 000 ft it is equal to 2 x weight (metric tons) + 80, and above you need to add 1 kt for every 1000 ft.

Vref: Equal to 1.23 Vs in CONF FULL (equal to VLS).

Vapp: Represents Vref+ΔVref+APPR corrections (with a correction limited to +20 kts —Airbus recommendation—). Procedure in QRH.

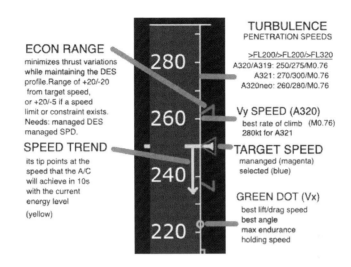

ECON RANGE

minimizes thrust variations while maintaining the DES profile.Range of +20/-20 from target speed, or +20/-5 if a speed limit or constraint exists. Needs: managed DES managed SPD.

SPEED TREND

its tip points at the speed that the A/C will achieve in 10s with the current energy level

(yellow)

TURBULENCE
PENETRATION SPEEDS

>FL200/>FL200/>FL320
A320/A319: 250/275/M0.76
A321: 270/300/M0.76
A320neo: 260/280/M0.76

Vy SPEED (A320)

best rate of climb   (M0.76)
280kt for A321

TARGET SPEED

mananged (magenta)
selected (blue)

GREEN DOT (Vx)

best lift/drag speed
best angle
max endurance
holding speed

SRS

The Speed Reference System (SRS) manages the A/C speed by changing the A/C pitch during takeoff and go around.

It commands:

- Takeoff: V2+10
- Takeoff SE: speed reached before failure, but at least V2.
- G/A: speed before G/A, but not less than Vapp.

SRS aims to achieve at least 120 fpm during climb.

On the ground, it is armed when V2 is inserted in the MCDU and the flap lever is above 0, and engaged by selecting FLX or TOGA. For all other phases, it engages by selecting TOGA with flap lever above 0. It needs 1FD or 1AP to be active.

KNOW YOUR FACTS...

- Flying with the A/THR active, even if the SPD Knob is pulled to a lower speed, speed will sit at VLS.

- EXPEDITE mode gives green dot during the climb and 340 kt during the descent.

- Do not change the database in flight. It will erase your current F-PLN and the ND will go blank!

AUTOFLIGHT — ABNORMAL

AUTO FLT - FCU 1(2) FAULT	At each baro setting change on the FCU, crosscheck the validity of both PFD altitude information with the SBY altimeter
AUTO FLT - RUD TRV LIM SYS	Rudder with care above 160 kts Use differential braking if needed Max X-wind: 15 kts
AUTO FLT - FAC1+2 FAULT	Rudder with care above 160 kts Alternate law
AUTO FLT - YAW DAMPER SYS	Both Daw yampers are lost Alternate law
SINGLE FMGC FAILURE	AP on the affected side will disconnect. Flight plan information on the affected ND may be recovered by using same range as the opposite ND. FMGC reset available
DUAL FMGC FAILURE	AP/FD/ATHR disconnect. RMPs used to tune navaids. FMGC reset available.

70

9. ELECTRICAL — 24

The A320 is powered by:

- Three-phase 115/200 V 400 Hz constant-frequency AC System

- 28 V DC System

Main components are:

- **AC Generators**: Engine-driven generators (90Kva, 115/200V, 400Hz), APU generator and external power. Additionally, the blue hydraulic circuit drives an emergency generator if all main generators fail (5Kva, 115/200V, 400Hz).

- **Static inverter**: transforms DC power from BAT1 into AC Power which supplies the AC ESS BUS. When the aircraft is above 50 kts the inverter is automatically activated if only BAT power is supplying the A/C.

- **Batteries**: with a normally capacity of 23 Ah, they are permanently connected to two hot buses. Each battery has an associated Battery Charge Limiter (BCL) which monitors battery charging and controls the battery contactor.

- **Transformer Rectifiers (TR)**: Two main rectifiers (TR1 and TR2) supply the aircraft with up to 200 A DC current. A third one (ESS TR) can power the essential DC circuit from the emergency generator.

The combination of each generator, together with its own constant speed drive and drive oil system is called Integrated Drive Generator (**IDG**)

TOP TIP! Should it be necessary to disconnect an IDG in flight, the disconnect P/B should be held for a maximum of 3 s, and only when the engine is running, otherwise the mechanism will be damaged.	

Let's see the schematic first during normal operation:

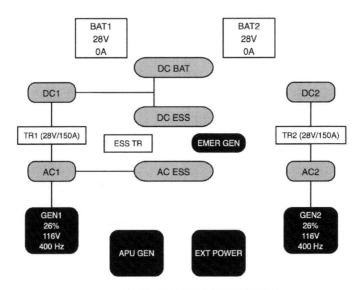

ELEC - NORMAL OPERATION

In **normal operation**, each engine-driven generator supplies its associated AC BUS via its generator line contactor (GLC1, GLC2). The Bus Tie Contactors (BTC) open or close to maintain power supply to both AC BUS. One. One contactor is closed when one ENG only and the APU are supplying the network (both closed during OE or APU or EXT PWR supply). *NOTE: GLC and BTC not in the picture above.*

AC BUS 1 normally supplies the AC ESS BUS, TR1 supplies DC BUS 1, DC BAT BUS and DC ESS BUS and TR2 supplies DC BUS 2.

The two batteries are connected to the DC BAT ESS if they need charging. When they are fully charged, the battery charge limiter disconnects them.

The **APU** Generator—as well as the **Ground Power**— might supply the whole system (AC BUS 1 and AC BUS 2). The APU might also share the load with one of the engine driven generators

See how the system works with some failures in the following pages:

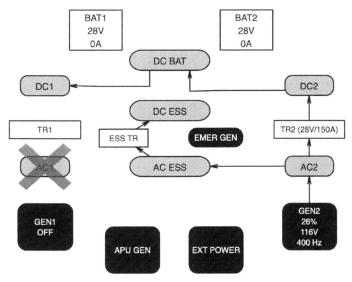

FAILURE OF AC BUS 1

If AC Bus 1 fails, AC ESS BUS is momentary loss. However, it can be restored by selecting the **AC ESS FEED PB**, which will enable AC BUS 2 to feed AC ESS (However, this is done automatically in newer A320). The rest of the configuration will be as shown in the picture above.

If <u>both</u> AC buses fail, the A/C will have to be supplied by the Emergency Generator (RAT).

Circuit breakers are color coded. Green circuit breakers are monitored by ECAM will give an ECAM MSG if pulled (C/B TRIPPED ON...)

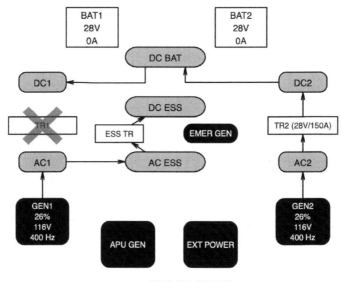

ONE TR FAULT

If TR1 or TR2 fail, their respective busses will automatically be fed through the DC BAT BUS by the opposite DC channel via the DC BUS TIE contractor.

If Both TR fail, DC1, DCBAT and DC2 remain unpowered. The only DC buses available are the HOT BAT and DC ESS buses.

Normal Priority
1. engine generators
2. external power
3. APU generator
4. RAT
5. Batteries

Commercial P/B disconnects:
1. cabin and cargo lights
2. Water and toilet system
3. Galleys
4. Pax entertainment system and in seat power supply
5. Drain mast ice protection

"Galy&Cab" P/B disconnects:
1. Main and secondary galley
2. In seat power supply

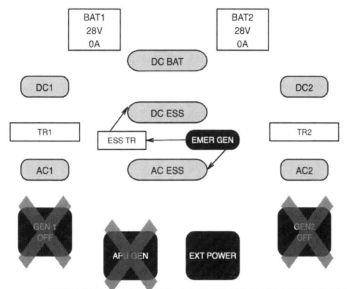

EMEGENCY GENERATOR - LOSS OF ALL MAIN GENERATORS

If all main generators fail, you will be left with the Emergency Generator (RAT), as both AC buses are lost. The RAT extends automatically if:

- o Speed is above 100 kts
- o Both AC buses are lost

RAT extension takes around 8 s, during which time the A/C is powered on batteries only. When the landing gear is extended, the system reverts to flying with batteries only.

GENERATOR 1 LINE

The Generator Line 1 P/B isolates GEN 1 from the electrical network. The GEN keeps running but it is only dedicated to the fuel pumps (one in each wing). It is used as part of the ELEC EMERG CONFIG.

ELECTRIC — ABNORMAL

ELEC - AC BUS 1 FAULT	Blower - OVRD // Blue hydraulic system is INOP
	Power must be rerouted to AC BUS 2. This is done automatically in newer A/C, but is achieved through the "AC ESS FEED" button in older ones.
ELEC - AC BUS 2 FAULT	Loss of FO's PFD and ND
	CAT 1 only
ELEC - DC BUS 1 FAULT	Blower and Extract - OVRD
	Avoid icing conditions
ELEC - DC BUS 2 FAULT	AIR DATA switch F/O 3
	Check baro reference on FCU
	CDLS inoperative
	Slats and flaps slow
	SEC2+3 inoperative — performance corrections needed
ELEC - AC ESS BUS FAULT	AC ESS FEED to ALTN
	ATC/XPDR to SYS2
	CP PFD and ND lost
	Loss of Pax Oxygen masks, so a descend will be needed. 25000 ft is a good compromise as "Time of useful consciousness" is around 2-3 minutes.
ELEC - DC ESS BUS FAULT	Wing anti-ice inoperative
	GPWS off/FCU1 lost.
	Blue Hydraulic system is inoperative.
	The major issue might be the loss of comms. VHF1, ACP1 and ACP2 are lost. Comms are recovered by AUDIO SWTG selector to ACP3, using VHF2/3. Loudspeaker 2 is the only one available.
	FCU1, GPWS, WAI and SFCC1 also lost.

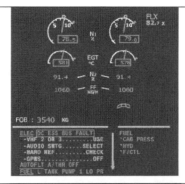

ELEC - EMER

CONFIG

This one of the most complicated failures in the A320. A lot of systems are lost when on Emergency Configuration. The QRH will give you an idea of the inop systems. It is very important to apply the Airbus Golden Rules (Fly, Navigate Communicate).

CP will take over the PF role as the FO is left with no screens. VHF1 only is available. Follow ECAM actions. Remember that you can start the APU on batteries below FL250.

Gravity fuel feeding is required.

For the APP, no RA calls are available and you will be in Direct Law.

TOP TIP!

It is highly recommended that, with an electrical failure, you check the "Required Equipment for CAT2/3" in the QRH

10. FLIGHT CONTROLS — 27

All flight control surfaces are electrically controlled and hydraulically activated.

The stabilizer and the rudder can also be mechanically-controlled.

Nine computers process pilot and autopilot inputs:

- 2 ELACs (Elevator Aileron Computer)
- 3 SECs (Spoilers Elevator Computer)
- 2 FACs (Flight Augmentation Computer)
- 2 FCDC (Flight Control Data Concentrators), which acquire data from the ELACs and the SECs and send it to the EIS and the CFDS.

FLAPS AND SLATS

Each wing has the following lift-augmentation devices:

- Two flap surfaces (double-slotted flap in A321)
- Five slat surfaces

The pilot extends slats and flaps by moving a single lever (FLAPS) only, having 5 different positions (0,1,2,3,FULL). For reference, CONF FULL equates to 35º in the A320, 40º in the A319 and 25º on the A321.

They are controlled by two Slat Flap Control Computers (**SFCC**). If only one SFCC is operative, the flaps and the slats will operate at half speed.

Flaps 1 is a "hybrid" configuration as it has two separate configurations for the same Flaps 1 handle position:

- o FLAP 1: slats only
- o FLAP 1+F: slats and flaps

The summary of its logic is that moving the flap lever to position "1" gives you CONF 1 on landing and 1+F in the rest of situations.

Flaps have an **overspeed protection** at setting 1+F at 210 IAS, flaps will automatically retract to Flap 1 only (thus leaving only the slats out). This protection becomes necessary in some cases. For instance, when operating an A321 at high gross take off weights, when "F" speed might be higher than 210 kts.

Slats have an **alpha lock** function that inhibits them from retracting from position 1 to 0 when the A/C is at high angle of attack or low airspeed.

Four Wingtip Brakes (WTB) lock the flaps or slats in case of asymmetry, overspeed, runaway or uncommanded movement. WTB's cannot be released in flight.

SIDESTICK

No feedback is given via the sidestick. Both sidesticks orders are algebraically summed. If both sidesticks are operated at the same time, a "DUAL INPUT" aural caution is heard.

A red Takeover P/B disconnect allows the pilot to override the other sidestick or to disable a damage sidestick. If priority is taken, then the audio "PRIORITY LEFT/RIGHT" sounds. A red arrow will then illuminate in front of the pilot who has been deactivated. A green CAPT or F/O light will illuminate in front of the pilot with priority of the sidestick is out of neutral.

Last pilot who presses the button has priority. However, pressing the PB for 40 s will latch the priority condition until the other PB is pressed.

CONTROL SURFACES AND COMPUTERS

In the following table you will the relationship between both:

Control Surface	Primary computer/ (back-up)	Function	Notes
Aileron	ELAC1 (ELAC2)	Roll	- Maximum deflection of ailerons is 25º - Ailerons extend 5º down when the flaps are extended (aileron droop) If both ELAC fail, ailerons revert to damping mode.
Spoilers	SECs	Speed-brake (S3,4,5) Roll (2,3,4,5) Ground (all) *Speed-brake auto-retrac-tion	- Maximum spoiler deflection for **roll** is 35º. - Maximum spoiler deflection for **braking**: • S3,4: 40º (manual), 25º (AP ON) • S2: 20º (manual), 12,5º (AP ON). The roll function has priority. A partial extension of the ground spoilers (10º) takes place when LDG, with at least IDLE rev, when one strut is compressed, in order to help the other main L/G touch the ground. If a SEC fails, the spoilers it controls are automatically retracted. Speedbrakes are inhibited when: • SEC1 and SEC3 fault • One elevator fault • AoA protection and Alpha Floor • Thrust Levers above MCT • Flaps CONF FULL (or CONF3 in A319/A321)*
Elevator	ELAC2 (ELAC1) (SEC1) (SEC2)	Pitch	- Maximum deflection is 30º NU, or 17º ND.
THS	ELAC2 (ELAC1) (SEC1) (SEC2)	Pitch	Powered by one of the three electric motors. Mechanical control is achieved through the trim wheel. It has priority over electrical control.
Rudder	ELAC1 FAC1 (FAC2)	Yaw	ELAC1: • turn coordination • dutch roll damping • sends orders to FAC. FAC1: • accomplishment of ELAC orders. • Rudder trim • Yaw in alternate law	Max deflection is 20º Rudder trim rates are: AP- 5º/sec MAN-1º/sec

F/CTL GENERAL ARCHITECTURE

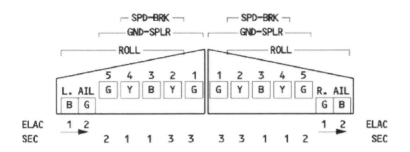

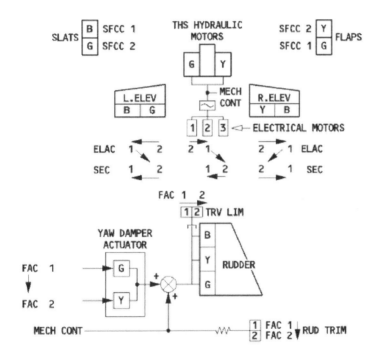

→ Arrows indicate the control reconfiguration priorities

G B Y indicates the hydraulic power source (green, blue, or yellow) for each servo control.

LOAD ALLEVIATION FUNCTION

the load alleviation function permits to alleviate the wing structure loads. It is achieved through the upward deflection of:

- Two ailerons only or
- The two ailerons associated to Spoilers 4 and 5 (in case of gust detection)

The LAF is available when the aircraft is in clean configuration and in normal law.

FLIGHT LAWS

	NORMAL LAW (green ` `)	**ALTERNATE LAW** (amber XX)
Ground mode	direct proportional relationship between sidestick deflection and F/CTRL.	
Flight mode	• Becomes active shortly after take off. • Sidestick deflection proportional to load factor. • Sidestick neutral maintains 1g load in pitch. • Sidestick roll input commands a roll rate request.	Load factor demand similar to normal law. Degrades to direct law when landing gear is extended. Automatic trim available Turn coordination is lost
Flare mode	• Transition to flare mode occurs at 50' RA • System memorizes pitch attitude at 50º and begins progressively to reduce pitch, forcing the pilot to flare the aircraft.	No flare mode (direct law)
Protec- tions	**LOAD FACTOR LIMITATION** Prevents pilot from overstresssing the A/C	All protections except for the load factor maneuvering protections are lost.

ATTITUDE PROTECTION

Pitch limited to 30º UP, 15º DN

Bank limited to 67º

Bank >33º requires constant input

With high AoA Protection, bank limited to 45º.

With High Speed Protection, bank limited to 40º and A/C returns to wings level.

HIGH AoA PROTECTION

When alpha exceeds alpha prot, elevator control switches to alpha protection mode in which AoA is proportional to sidestick deflection.

ALpha max will not be exceeded even if the pilot applies full aft deflection. Without pilot input, the A/C speed will sit at Alpha Prot.

HIGH SPEED PROTECTION

Starts at Vmo+4 kts and Mmo+0,006 (green ``)

Prevents exceeding Vmo or Mmo introducing a pitch up load factor demand which can be overriden by the pilot. Once past Vmo+15 kts or Mmo+0,04 the pilot pitch-up

Load factor limitation is similar to normal law.

LOW SPEED STABILITY

Nose down command when between 5-10 kts close to Vsw, that can be overridden by the pilot.

Alpha floor inoperative

A/C can be stalled.

HIGH SPEED STABILITY

Nose up demand when exceeding Vmo/Mmo, which can be overridden.

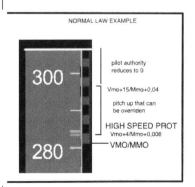

NORMAL LAW EXAMPLE

authority smoothly reduces to zero.

LOW ENERGY WARNING

Available in CONF2,3 or FULL between 100' and 2000' RA when TOGA not selected. "SPEED SPEED SPEED" sounds when thrust is needed to recover a positive flight path (pitch change not sufficient).

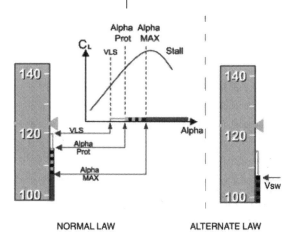

NORMAL LAW   ALTERNATE LAW

The checked band between V alpha prot and Alpha Max is black and orange, whereas the one below it is fully red.

The checked band below Vsw is red and black.

DIRECT LAW

Direct relationship between sidestick and control surface

No auto-trimming

"USE MAN PITCH TRIM" in amber message.

No protections but stall aural warning provided.

MECHANICAL BACKUP

In this mode, pitch is provided through horizontal stab trim, and lateral control through the rudder and differential power. Both stab and rudder use cables and require hydraulic power.

"MAN PITCH TRIM ONLY" in red appears.

Mechanical backup is not designed to fly the A/C, but to keep it in the air while other systems are recovered.

FLIGHT CONTROLS — ABNORMAL

F/CTL - FLAPS /SLATS FAULT/LOCKED	Speed is limited to the VFE corresponding to the next more extended flap configuration. When the failure comes up, **PULL SPEED!** When speed below VFE, recycle flap lever. Apply QRH procedure. For APP configuration, you will have to select SPD VFE NEXT -5 kt until LDG CONFIG. Pay attention to the table provided for go-around speeds. Flaps/Slats position are the ones indicated by the E/WD. note: VLS is based on actual flap position, so it can be trusted. Be aware fuel consumption will increase dramatically!

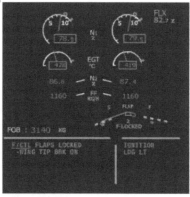

F/CTL - SPLR FAULT	If S3, S4 affected, do not use speedbrakes Apply necessary corrections
F/CTL - SPD BRK FAULT	Ground spoilers available through reverse application on landing.
F/CTL - RUDDER JAM	Max X-wind 15 kts, and avoid wind from the side where the rudder is deflected.

	Do not use autobrake.
F/CTL - L (R) ELEV FAULT	Alternate law Max speed 320 kts Apply necessary performance corrections If **both** are lost, pitch reverts to mechanical back up and roll to direct law.
F/CTL - STAB JAM	Alternate law If manual pitch available, maintain elevator at 0 position. L/G down recommended at LDG CONFIG.
F/CTL - SEC FAULT	Normally reset offered first. If all SEC inop, alternate law
F/CTL - ELAC FAULT	Normally reset offered first If both ELAC affected, ailerons lost and alternate law.
F/CTL - FCFC1+2 FAULT	F/CTL indications on ECAM are lost, together with bank and pitch limits, V alfa prot and MAX. Vsw is lost and the stall warning may sound. Normal law is kept.
SIDESTICK FAULT	Uncommanded control inputs could be consequence of a sidestick fault. Generally speaking, the A/P will fail if this happens and the A/C will move as if the input was intentional. The A/C should be recoverred with the other sidestick, by pressing the takeover button for 40s, thus locking the other sidestick. The A/P can be re-engaged again. *Note: do not disconnect the A/P with the takeover button as the failed sidestick will be reintroduced into the system. Use the FCU instead.*

11. FUEL — 28

The A320 stores its fuel in:

- One center tank under the aircraft belly
- The wings' inner tank
- The wings' outer tank

There is a vent surge tank outboard of the outer tank in each wing. Fuel can expand by 2 % without spilling when the aircraft has been filled to its maximum capacity.

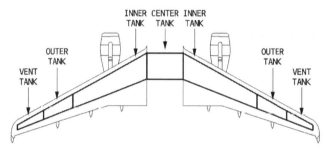

The approximate fuel capacity of the A320 (although it is variable) is around:

Outer tanks	700 kg
Inner tanks	5500 kg
Centre tank	6500 kg
Total	**18900** kg

Fuel feed sequence

The inner tanks feed the fuel to the engines and empty in the following sequence:

- Centre tanks.
- Inner tanks: tank empties down to 750kg ECAM MSG: **OUTER TK FUEL XFRD** appears
- Outer tanks: Fuel transfers into the inner tanks

NOTE1: Center tank pumps are deactivated with Slats OUT to prevent the A/C using Center Tanks Fuel during T/O. During that phase, high pressure is required and 4 pumps are available for the inner tanks against 2 only from the Centre tanks.

NOTE2: New A320s (>2014) are equipped with jet pumps and transfer valves. Fuel in the Center tanks is transferred to the inner tanks.

Transfer valves

Two electrical transfer valves are mounted in each wing to permit fuel transfer from outer to inner tanks.

Cross feed valve

A cross feed valve allows both engines to be fed from both sides.

Suction valves

Closed by pumps in normal operation, they allow engines to be fed by gravity if necessary.

Fuel recirculation

Some of the fuel supplied to each engine goes from the high-pressure fuel line in that engine, through the integrated drive generator (IDG) heat exchanger (where it absorbs heat) to the fuel return valve, and then to the outer fuel tank. The fuel return valve is controlled by the FADEC.

Refueling

Refueling is normally automatic, although a manual operation is also possible. Automatic refueling starts normally by the outer cells. When an outer cell is full, fuel normally overflows into the inner cell through a spill pipe. Refuel valves close automatically when the preselected value is reached.

Fuel indication

FQI (Fuel Quantity Indication) System: is a computerized system that transmits the total actual fuel mass to the ECAM and controls automatic refuelling. Fuel quantity is calculated via a set of capacitance probes and densitometers.

FLSCU (Fuel Level Sensing Control Unit): it generates fuel-level and fuel-temperature signals in order to assist refuelling and control the IDG cooling system. It triggers the LO LVL warning on ECAM.

$$5030$$

The last two digits of the fuel figure will have an **amber line** when FQI information is inaccurate.

A **box** will appear around the number when that fuel is unusable. A half-box will appear around the total FOB when a portion of it is unusable.

A321 differences

The A321 center tank does not have the same pumps, but use jet pumps instead, same as the new A320s. The A321 Wing Tanks do not have an outer and inner tank and there are no transfer valves.

APU feed

the APU has a special fuel pump that works when fuel feed pressure is low. It runs off the AC ESS SHED or the AC STAT INV BUS.

KNOW YOUR FACTS...

- Approximate refueling time is 20 minutes for all tanks, 17 for wing tanks only.
- There is ECAM OUTR TK FUEL XFRD memo on the A321 as there is no outer or inner wing tank. However, there is a memo of "FOB below 3T".

FUEL — ABNORMAL

FUEL - GRAVITY FEEDING	This procedure may be required if there is an issue with the fuel pumps. First of all, altitude at which the event triggers is really important, as it will determine your MAX FL. It might vary from A/C to A/C but as a guideline: • Ceiling FL300 if <30 min above FL300. • Ceiling = current FL if >30 min above FL300. • Ceiling FL150 or 7000 ft above take off airport (highest) if FL300 never exceeded. The wisest approach to the issue would be to maintain the FL at which the alert is triggered. As you can see, probably you will have to descend to a lower level. Use the QRH procedure.
FUEL - "X"* TK HI TEMP	*where "X" is any of the fuel tanks.* On ground: delay take off, engine off. In flight: • Fuel T > 60ºC O/T, 54ºC I/T: increase FF + • Fuel T >65ºC O/T, 57ºC I/T: APU start + • If opposite IDG operative, turn off affected IDG. *I/T: inner tank, O/T: outer tank*
FUEL IMBALANCE	A fuel imbalance may occur for several reasons (operational, Single Engine, Leak...). Therefore, it is imperative that before the flight crew initiates the QRH procedure, they confirm that no leak is affecting the A/C. Take into account that the advisory threshold is 1500 kg difference between two tanks. However, handling is ensured even in case of maximum difference.
FUEL LEAK	First identify the source of the fuel leak by reference to the QRH procedure, checking the SD page.

Consider immediate diversion options.

If a leak is confirmed, the QRH has two different scenarios:

- Leak confirmed from pylon/engine — shut down the engine to isolate the fuel leak
- Leak source not confirmed — Isolate each tank to check depletion rate from each tank

Do not open the Fuel X-Feed unless you are absolutely sure you can do so.

Once the fuel leak is confirmed, a diversion must be initiated. Consider a possible SE approach and fire services on the ground. A fuel leak may cause fire upon landing.

12. HYDRAULICS — 29

The aircraft has three continuously operating hydraulic systems: blue, green and yellow. Each system has its own reservoir. All systems have a normal operating pressure of 3000 PSI, except when the blue one is operated by the RAT (2 500 PSI). Hydraulic fluid cannot be transferred from one system to the other.

Green system pump

A pump drive by engine 1 pressurizes the green system

Blue system pump

An electric pump pressurizes the blue system.

In emergency cases, a pump driven by a ram air turbine (RAT) pressurizes the system.

Yellow system pumps

A pump driven by engine 2 pressurizes the yellow system.

An electric pump can also pressurize the yellow system, which allows yellow hydraulics to be used on the ground when the engines are stopped.

Crew members can also use a hand pump to pressurize the yellow system in order to operate cargo doors when no electrical power is available.

PTU — Power Transfer Unit

A bidirectional power transfer unit enables the yellow system to pressurize the green system and viceversa. It comes into action automatically when the difference in pressure between both systems is greater than 500 PSI.

Accumulators

An accumulator in each system helps to maintain a constant pressure by covering transient demands during normal operation.

Priority valves

They cut off hydraulic power to heavy load users if hydraulic pressure in a system gets low.

Let's begin with the schematic of the hydraulic system:

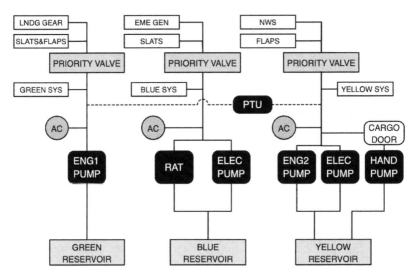

AC = accumulator
GREEN/BLUE/YELLOW SYS = it refers to a group of systems that are not described in the picture. You can see some of these systems in a table in Chapter 10 (Flight Controls). On top of these, REV1 is powered by the Green System and REV2 by the Yellow one.

HYDRAULICS — INDICATIONS AND ECAM

HYDRAULIC — ECAM

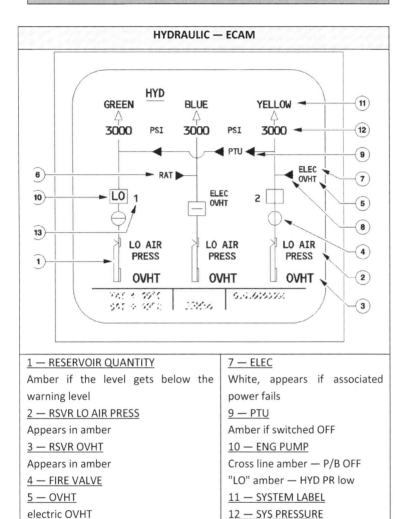

1 — RESERVOIR QUANTITY	7 — ELEC
Amber if the level gets below the warning level	White, appears if associated power fails
2 — RSVR LO AIR PRESS	9 — PTU
Appears in amber	Amber if switched OFF
3 — RSVR OVHT	10 — ENG PUMP
Appears in amber	Cross line amber — P/B OFF
4 — FIRE VALVE	"LO" amber — HYD PR low
5 — OVHT	11 — SYSTEM LABEL
electric OVHT	12 — SYS PRESSURE
6 — RAT	Amber when Pr < 1450 psi

HYDRAULICS — ABNORMAL

HYD G/Y RSVR LO AIR PR	This alert triggers when the reservoir air pressure is at or below 22 PSI The ECAM asks to turn the PUMP and the PTU OFF if PR fluctuates. NOTE: the probability of cavitation increases with altitude. Therefore, it may be possible to restore the system after descending to a lower altitude.
HYD G/Y RSVR LO LVL	This alert triggers when the fluid quantity is below 3.5 l (0.92 US gallons). The ECAM asks to turn the PUMP and the PTU OFF
HYD G/Y RSVR OVT	This alert triggers when the fluid temperature is above 93ºC. The ECAM asks to turn the PUMP and the PTU OFF

DUAL HYDRAULIC FAILURES

They are one of the most complex failures in the A320 and require good ECAM management .

PROCEDURES	SYSTEMS FAILED
GREEN AND YELLOW	
Be established at Vapp and LDG CONF before L/G down. F3 - Vapp = Vref+25 kt BRK Yellow Acc only	ALT LAW AP1/2 THS Stuck Slats slow, Flaps inop No L/G retraction No NSW Steering

GREEN AND BLUE	
L/G Gravity Extension at 200 kt (Max improved control speed at 195 kt). F3 - Vapp=Vref+25 kt No speedbrake *CAUTION! if blue lost by elec. pump - RAT is available for hyd. press!*	ALT LAW AP1/2+A/THR Ailerons inop Slats inop, flaps slow No L/G retraction
BLUE AND YELLOW	
F-FULL Landing *CAUTION! if blue lost by elec. pump - RAT is available for hyd. press!*	NORMAL LAW AP1/2 inop Slats and Flaps slow No NSW Steering

KNOW YOUR FACTS...

- The BLUE system is powered during first ENG start
- RAT extension status can be found in ECAM HYD page.
- Gravity Extension Handcrank requires 3 turns clockwise.
- Accumulator supplies at least 7 applications on braking.
- Hydraulic Power is cut off to the LDG when SPD>260 kt.

13. ICE&RAIN— 30

Icing conditions exist when the OAT (on the ground or close to the ground) or TAT (in flight) is at or below 10º C and visible moisture (such as clouds, rain or fog with visibility <1600m) is present.

Engine anti-ice uses hot air from independent bleed from the HP compressor. If electrical power is lost, the valves fail in the open position.

Wing Anti-Ice heats the three outer wing slat panels on each wing. APU bleed should not be used for anti-icing due to the lack of temperature control.

Both sides windows and the windscreen are electrically heated. This operates whenever one engine is running, although less power is applied on the ground. This is controlled by the PROBE/WINDOW HEAT PB on the overhead panel. The heating operates at high power when airborne.

For take-off purposes, a **damp runway** is the one whose surface is not dry, but moisture does not give a shiny appearance. For performance reasons, a damp runway is considered as a wet runway.

If the whole runway is identified as "**slippery** when wet", in your EFB calculations, select:

- ICY, when OAT is at or below 5º C
- STANDING water 12.7 mm when above.

If only a portion is identified as "slippery when wet", the flight crew can subtract the affected portion off the total runway length by using the EFB performance module. Then consider the rest of the runway as "wet".

TOP TIP!

Vibration can indicate icing building up in the engine.

Maybe you forgot to switch the engine anti-ice on...

KNOW YOUR FACTS...

- Drain masts are heated whenever there is electrical power to the A/C.
- Wing anti-ice available for OEI (if fire P/B not pushed) by using pack off and crossbleed open.
- Probes are heated whenever there is at least one engine running
- If landing under icing conditions, the anti-ice PB should be turned off when the aircraft is on stand.
- When engine anti-ice is ON, max N1 is limited, ignition comes ON and the min engine RPM are increased.

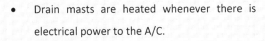

DOUBLE AOA HEAT FAILURE (QRH)	In the case of double failure of alpha probe heaters, the choice made by the computers among 3 ADR might be erroneous. ONE OF THE AFFECTED ADR is asked to be OFF, preferably not ADR1. In the case of disagreement between the two remaining ADRs, the NAV ADR DISAGREE alert might trigger.
[ANTI-ICE] 2 pitot tubes [ANTI-ICE] ALL PITOT	If two or even all pitot tubes are affected by icing, the ECAM will look for erroneous data. Caution, because two pitot tubes could be presenting equal but wrong data. Be prepared to apply the UNRELIABLE SPD PROC.
[ANTI-ICE] 2 AoA	In case 2 AoA probes give incorrect data, the A/C might consider them as accurate and isolate the third one. The following ECAM procedure avoids that the flight controls use erroneos data: ADR 1(2) PB .... OFF In case of subsequent and significant AOA discrepancy between the two remaining ADR, the "NAV ADR DISAGREE" ECAM might trigger.
[ANTI-ICE] only one side failed (pitot/probe)	If only one side (CPT/FO/SBY) is failed, be it the Aoa probe or the pitot tube, crew must select the AIR DATA SWTG in order to get the correct information.

14. LANDING GEAR — 32

The landing gear consists of two main landing gears and one nose landing gear.
Gear and doors are electrically controlled and hydraulically operated.

Two Landing Gear Control and Inferface Units (**LGCIUs**) control the extension
and the retraction of the gear and the operation of the doors. They also supply
information about the landing gear to ECAM for display. One LGCIU controls a
complete gear cycle, then switches to the other LGCIU.

If the normal system fails to extend the landing gear hydraulically, the flight crew
can use a crank to extend it mechanically. When a crew member turns the crank,
it:

1) Isolates de landing gear hydraulics

2) Unlocks the gear doors

3) Allows gravity to drop the gear.

The main wheels are equipped with carbon multidisc brakes, which can be
actuated by two independent brakes systems, with three different
combinations:

- **Normal system**: uses green hydraulic pressure, it has got an antiskid
  system and is controlled by the Brake and Steering Control Unit
  (BSCU).

- **Alternate system with antiskid**: using the yellow hydraulic system,
  although the braking is controlled by the Alternate Braking Control
  Unit (ABCU).

- **Alternate system without antiskid**: same as before, but without using
  antiskid. If the accumulator is available, braking pressure is
  automatically limited to 1000 PSI for a maximum of seven
  applications.

Remember, with normal braking there will be no pressure indication.

Normal brake pressure is between 2000 and 2700 psi.

Brake temperature

Take-off is normally not allowed if temperature is above 300ºC (lower for some airlines), or 150ºC if brake fans have been used.

Maintenance is needed if:

- The temperature difference between two brakes in the same gear is above 150ºC, and one of them is above 600º or below 60º C.
- The temperature difference between the LH and the RH brakes average temperature is around 200ºC or more.
- A single brake temperature exceeds 900ºC.
- A fuse plug has melted.

Auto brake

The crew may arm the system by pressing the LO, MED or MAX pushbutton provided all the following arming conditions are met:

- ○ Green pressure available
- ○ Anti-skid electrically powered
- ○ No failure in the braking system
- ○ At least one ADIRU available

Auto brake is activated when:

- o   for LO and MED: The command for ground spoiler extension is detected, with a delay of 4s for LO and 2s for MED. The deceleration rate is 1.7 m/s for LO and 3 m/s for MED.
- o   for MAX: the command for ground spoilers is detected and wheel speed is above 40 kt.

Therefore, during a rejected take-off, if the aircraft begins to decelerate before reaching 72 kt, the automatic braking will not activate because the ground spoilers will not extend.

Nose Wheel Steering

NWS gets inputs from:

- both the CPT and the F/O steering hand wheels. Max deflection is 75º and starts reducing above 20 kts to be 0º at 70 kts.
- Rudder pedals, with max deflection of 6º, reducing to 0º at 130 kts (above 40 kts).
- Autopilot

A green NW SRG DISC message will show on ECAM and will turn amber on second engine start when lever is activated.

Anti-skid

When the anti-skid system detects that the tyre speed is reduced to around 0.87 times the A/C speed, a servo valve releases the brakes.

LANDING GEAR — ABNORMAL

If the crew suspects that there is a problem with the landing gear, the L/G GRAVITY EXTENSION and the LDG WITH ABNORMAL L/G QRH procedures may be disregarded if there is at least one green triangle on each landing gear:

Symbol ▽	Symbol ▼	Landing Gear Position
Green	Green	Both systems detect gear downlock.
Green	Red	One system detects gear downlock; the other detects gear in transit.
Green	No Symbol	One system detects gear downlock; the other detects gear uplock.
Red	Red	Both systems detect gear in transit.
Red	No Symbol	One system detects gear in transit; the other detects gear uplock.
No Symbol	No Symbol	Both systems detect gear uplock.

This is confirmed too by the "LDG GEAR DN" green memo. Disregard any "TOO LOW GEAR" aural alert if it comes up.

TOP TIP!

Do not use the AUTOBRAKE and switch the anti-skid off if landing with any or both of the landing gears in abnormal position. The reference speed used by the anti-skid system will not be correct.

TOP TIP!!

Switch the engines off just before touch down if abnormal position in the landing gear. Hydraulic power will be available up to 30s after this.

LANDING GEAR — ABNORMAL

L/G - GRAVITY EXTENSION	Pull and turn the gravity extension handle and pull down landing gear lever.
L/G - GEAR NOT DOWN	This warning triggers when: • L/G not downlocked and RA<750 with both engines N1<75 %. • L/G not downlocked and RA<750 ft and both engines are not at T/O power and FLAPS out. • L/G not downlocked and F3 or F-FULL, and both RA failed.
L/G - GEAR NOT UPLOCKED	If landing gear **not downlocked**: • Maximum speed: VLO • Recycle landing gear • If unsuccessful, landing gear down If landing gear **downlocked**: • Maximum speed: VLE If landing gear doors closed and landing not **uplocked**: • Avoid excessive g load factor
L/G - GEAR UPLOCK FAULT	Maximum speed VLE Keep L/G down
L/G - SHOCK ABSORBER FAULT	If landing gear not uplocked, max speed is VLE. Keep L/G down.
L/G - DOORS NOT CLOSED	When speed is below VLO, recycle L/G. If unsuccessful, maximum speed VLO.
BRAKES - A-SKID N-WS FAULT or OFF	Maximum pressure: 1000 PSI NWS inoperative

105

L/G - LGCIU 1(2) FAULT	If LGCIU 1 fails, GPWS is failed. Losing LGCIU 1 you will lose as well the indications next to the L/G lever. APPR IDLE ONLY AND REVERSER MIGHT BE INOP
L/G - LGCIU 1+2	GPWS Lost L/G via gravity extension APPR IDLE ONLY CAT 1 only AP lost A/THR is lost N/W STR lost in some A/C
WHEEL - NWS FAULT	It triggers when the NWS is failed. CAT3 single only. CAUTION: if the L/G SHOCK ABSORBER FAULT is also displayed, then the NW may be at maximum deflection (90º).
WHEEL TIRE DAMAGE SUSPECTED	LDG DIST must be applied. Performance impact of one burst tire is equivalent to one brake released. (QRH procedure)
RESIDUAL BRAKING	Should be checked shortly after every gear extension (some residual braking is acceptable right after gear down selection). If residual pressure exists, try to zero it by pressing the pedals. If it persists, select "MED" autobrake in order to prioritize normal braking before alternate braking.

15. NAVIGATION —34— AND ECAM

ADIRS

The Air Data and Inertial Reference Systems (ADIRS) supplies temperature, anemometric, barometric and inertial parameters to the EFIS system (PFD and ND) and to other user systems.

The system includes:

- Three **ADIRUs**, divided in two parts: an **ADR** part providing barometric altitude, airspeed, Mach, angle of attack, temperature and overspeed warnings, and an **IR** part, supplying attitude, flight path vector, track, heading, accelerations, angular rates, ground speed and aircraft position.

- One ADIRS control panel.

- Four types of sensors: Pitot probes (3), Static pressure probes (STAT) (6), Angle of attack sensors (AOA) (3), Total air temperature probes (2). These sensors are electrically heated to prevent from icing up.

- Eight ADM (Air Data Module), which convert pneumatic data from PITOT and STAT probes into numerical data for the ADIRUs.

ADIRU controls in the overhead panel.

NOTE: The order of the ADIRUs is 1/3/2, and not 1/2/3 as one might expect!

NOTE: The "IR" section is turned off by selecting "OFF" with the rotary knob. The "ADR" section is selected "OFF" by pushing its pushbutton.

The IR "ATT" option may recover HDG and Attitude information (only if FAULT light flashing). However, magnetic heading must be entered via the ADIRS control panel and updated frequently.

GPS

The Global Positioning System is a satellite-based navigation using 24 satellites. Data is transferred to the ADIRUs, which compute a GPS-IRS hybrid position.

NAVAIDS

The aircraft has:

- Two VOR receivers.

- Two ILS/GLS/MLS receivers. PFD1 and ND2 display ILS1 information. PFD2 and ND1 display ILS2 information.

- ADF: may be fitted with one or two ADF.

- DME: has two DMEs. and their frequency is automatically set to the frequency/channel that is set on the VOR or ILS.

NAVIGATION

Each FMGC computes its own aircraft position (called the "FM position") from a MIX IRS position and a computed radio position, or a GPS position.

- MIX IRS position: computed as a weighted average of all IRs.

- GPS-IRS position: mixing de IRS position with GPS data.

- Radio position: each FMGC uses onside navaids to compute its radio position (DME/DME, VOR/DME, LOC...).

The final position is based on one of the following modes, the first one having priority:

- IRS-GPS

- IRS-DME/DME

- IRS-VOR/DME

- IRS only.

The A320 works as well on a vector called the "**bias**". Each FMGC computes continuously a vector that goes from the MIX IRS position to the GPIRS position or the radio position. In case external data is lost, the bias is memorized and used to update the MIX IRS position whilst external data is recovered.

The full **alignment** of the inertial reference system (IRS) takes around 10 min, and the short one around 30 s.

POSITION ACCURACY

The FMGS continuously computes an Estimated Position Uncertainty (EPU), and compares it with the Required Navigation Performance (RNP):

- NAV Accuracy HIGH: EPU < RNP
- NAV Accuracy LOW: RNP > EPU

IRS-GPS is normally the most accurate position, giving an EPU of around 0.05 NM. Radio position is normally well below 0.50 NM. IRS only position, however, drifts enormously with time with 6 NM of EPA in the first 40 min, reaching around 10 NM EPA in 2 hours and around 2 NM extra per hour for the remainder of the flight *(see FCOM 22_20-20-20)*.

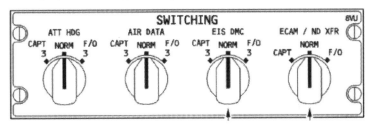

ECAM

The ECAM (Electronic Centralized Aircraft Monitoring) system is made up of:

- 2 SDACs (System Data Acquisition Concentrators)
- 2 FWCs (Flight Warning Computers).

A loss of one of this systems will not result in any loss of functions.

The SDACs receive data and send it to 3 different DMC (Display Management Computer), which generate the screen image. The FWC will generate the warning/caution messages.

The E/WD (Engine/Warning Display) shows normal engine readings, flap settings, memo messages and ECAM messages. The SD is directly below it and shows system pages or status.

The E/WD has priority over the SD, so if the upper display fails, the E/WD is automatically transferred to the lower display. If this occurs, the crew can manually select a system screen by pressing and holding the required key on the ECAM control panels. The SD can also be transferred to the CPT or F/O's ND by using the ECAM/ND XFER switching facility.

The ECAM uses the following colour codes:

- @   RED — immediate action.
- @   AMBER — awareness.
- @   GREEN — normal operation.
- @   PULSING GREEN — abnormal parameter
- @   WHITE — titles and remarks
- @   BLUE — action to be carried out.
- @   MAGENTA — special message.

ECAM management is dealt with in section 21.

FLIGHT PHASES

The A320 works on different flight phases. This is important, for instance, because each one of them is associated with a specific piece of information in the SD page:

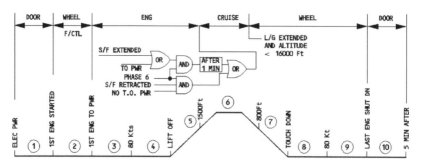

The A320 has a T/O and a LDG inhibit where most ECAM cautions are inhibited.
They are active:

- T/O: ground to 1500 ft
- LDG: 800 ft to ground.

T/O CONFIG PUSHBUTTON

When it is pushed or takeoff power is applied, a warning is triggered if the A/C
is not properly configured for takeoff. If it is, the "T.O. CONFIG NORMAL"
message will display green in the ECAM MEMO.

The following messages may be generated if the aircraft is not properly
configured for takeoff:

- CONFIG SLATS (FLAPS) NOT IN T.O. RANGE
- CONFIG PITCH NOT IN T.O. RANGE
- CONFIG SPD BRK NOT RETRACTED
- CONFIG RUD TRIM NOT IN T.O. RANGE
- CONFIG L/R) SIDESTICK FAULT
- BRAKES HOT
- DOORS
- CONFIG PARK BRAKE ON
- ENF FLEX TEMP NOT SET

EMER CANC PUSHBUTTON

Cancels only aural signals for warnings and cancels all cautions for the
remainder of the flight. They can be retrieved by pressing the RCL P/B for 3s.

KNOW YOUR FACTS...

- If the IR alignment countdown stops one minute before its accomplishment and the ALIGN lights start flashing, you forgot to enter position data in the FMGS.

- ILS1 displays its information in PFD1 and ND2.

- Wind information will not show up on your ND until you have reached 100kt.

NAVIGATION — ABNORMAL

NOTE: apply the UNRELIABLE AIRSPEED memory item at any point if there is any

doubt about speed reliability and the flight path might be compromised.

NAV - RA1+2 FAULT	When gear down — direct law *CAUTION: this fault goes directly from normal law to direct* *law upon gear extension.* *note: loss of ILS APPR capability, so LOC/FPA only.*
NAV - IR 1+2 FAULT *(or any* *other* *combination)*	Alternate law, direct law when gear down Use ATT HDG as appropriate *NOTE: with an IR fault, do not switch off the IR, as it will* *switch off the corresponding ADR too!*
NAV - ADR 1+2 FAULT *(or any* *other* *combination)*	Alternate law, direct law when gear down Use AIR DATA switching as appropriate
NAV - ADR 1+2+3	This procedure requires the flight crew to turn off the three ADRs and use the Back Up Scale (BUSS) and GPS altitude. If triple fault not detected by ECAM, it might show as double ADR fault only. A/C is in alternate law, direct law for landing. (QRH procedure)
NAV - IR DISAGREE	Direct law Use standby horizon to determine the faulty IR If faulty IR identified, turn it off. Then reset the ELACs and alternate law is recovered.
NAV - ADR DISAGREE	Alternate law Use both PFDs and standby airspeed indicator to determine the faulty ADR.

16. POWERPLANT —70—

The engine is a dual-rotor, variable stator, high by-pass ratio turbofan powerplant for subsonic services. They are control by a Full Authority Digital Engine Control (FADEC) that provides full engine management.

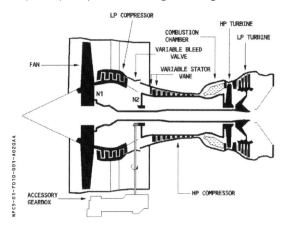

CFM example

The engine has:

- Two compressor turbine assemblies (High Pressure and Low Pressure)
- One accessory gearbox
- One combustion chamber

The **accessory gearbox** drives various accessories with mechanical power via de HP shaft. Each engine gearbox operates:

- The oil feed pump
- Main engine fuel pump
- Engine-driven hydraulic pumps

- Engine-driver generators
- FADEC alternator
- Pneumatic starter that enables engine start

FADEC

Each powerplant has a **FADEC** (Full Authority Digital Engine Control). Each FADEC has a two-channel redundancy, with one channel active and one in standby. FADECs are powered by their own magnetic alternator when the N2 increases above 10 %, or by the aircraft electrical system when the A/C electrical system decreases below 15 %.

The Engine Interface Unit (**EIU**) transmits to the FADEC the data that it (the FADEC) requires for engine management. Data is taken, from instance, from the Zone Controllers, the LGCIU or, in the A320$_{neos}$, from the BMC and the FCU.

The fuel flows from the tank, via the fuel pump and to the fuel/oil exchanger, then to the Hydromechanical Unit (**HMU**) and finally to the fuel nozzles (20 nozzles, 10 used normally and the other 10 according to the demand). The HMU controls de Fuel Flow, protects against overspeeding and controls fuel hydraulic signals to the actuators.

The FADEC carries many **functions**, which include:

- Fuel flow control and fuel recirculation
- Protection against limit exceedance (N1, N2, overspeed, EGT during start)
- Power management
- Automatic engine start
- Manual engine start (only start valve, HP valve, ignition)
- Thrust reverser

The FADEC has three different **idle** modes:

- Modulated idle: used on the ground —except when reverse is selected— and in flight when flaps are retracted.
- Approach idle: selected in flight when flaps are extended. It allows the engine to accelerate rapidly from idle to go-around thrust.
- Reverse idle: selected on the ground when thrust selected in REV IDLE position. It is slightly higher than the forward idle thrust.

The FADEC will abort a **start** for the following reasons:

- Hot start
- Hung start
- No light off
- Stalled engine

NOTE: if during a start a leak from the engine drain mast is reported, run the ENG at idle for 5 min. If the leak disappears, the A/C is dispatchable.

ENG START SEQUENCE

Normal start	Manual start
IGN START	IGN START
MASTER SWITCH ON	MAN START P/B ON
16 % IGN ON	min 20 % N2, ENG MASTER ON
22 % FUEL FLOW ON	Fuel and ignition begin
50 % START VALVE CLOSES	around 58 % N2, MAN START OFF
ENG MODE SEL - NORM	ENG MODE SEL - NORM

N2 background greys out during start and return to normal when stabilized.

Ignition A or B show during normal start, but A and B together when manual starting.

Manual start is advisable when:

- Aborting a start due to high EGT, ENG stall, LO START AIR PRESS, No N1 rotation or hung start.

- An unsuccessful start might be expected due to degraded bleed performance —high altitude, hot conditions—, marginal performance of the external pneumatic power group or tailwind greater than 10 kt.

The FADEC has limited authority during manual starting: it opens the start valve, it controls the position of the HP fuel valve and both igniters and it closes the start valve when N2 is at 50 % and it cuts the ignition off (on the ground only).

APU

The APU can supply electrical power up to 39 000 ft and air bleed from 20 000 ft downwards. If it is to be started on batteries, then it shall be started below 25 000 ft.

APU is not permitted for wing anti-ice.

APU is fed via the left fuel manifold. Therefore, the left tank will deplete at a faster rate than the right one when APU is ON.

When the APU Master Switch is selected ON, a self-test is completed, intake flap is open and fuel pressured is supplied.

The APU is ready for bleed and electrics when its power goes above 95 % for two seconds, or when it goes above 99,5 %.

When turning the APU OFF, it continues to run for a cooling period of 2 minutes.

Do not switch the batteries OFF before the APU flap shows fully closed.

POWERPLANT — INDICATIONS AND ECAM

POWERPLANT — ECAM

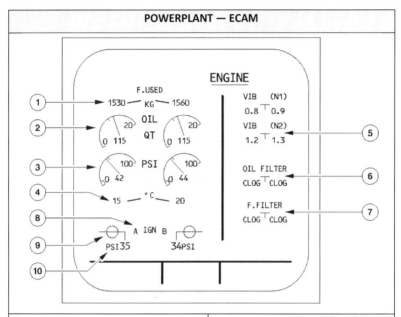

1 — FUEL USED	6 — OIL FILTER CLOG
reset with engine start	Amber if excessive P loss across the main
2 — OIL QUANTITY	oil scavenge filter.
3 — OIL PRESSURE	7 — FUEL FILTER CLOG
pulses if > 90 psi, or < 16 psi.	Amber if excessive P loss across the fuel
red if < 13 psi	filter.
4— OIL TEMPERATURE	8 — IGNITION
pulses if > 140º C	Active during start sequence
Amber if > 155 ºC, or > 140º C for more than	9 — START VALVE POSITION
15 minutes.	10 — ENGINE BLEED PR.
5 — VIBRATIONS	Amber when PR < 21 psi or there is an
pulses if N1 > 6, N2 > 4.3	overpressure.

POWERPLANT — ABNORMAL

ENG ABNORMAL RESPONSE	Some engine malfunctions might not trigger an ECAM alert and require some knowledge and analysis from the flight crew. When identifying an abnormal parameter, the crew should use all the available information. For instance, if FADEC fails and engine parameters are not shown, moving the THR levers should give us an indication whether the engine is alive or not, in case there is any doubt. All flight crews should aim to keep the engine running in flight. Even if the engine runs at idle power, it still powers the hydraulic, electric and bleed systems. Regardless of ECAM cautions or indications, the flight crew might suspect and engine failure if any of the following happens: • Increase of EGT above the red line • Important mismatch of the rotor speeds • Absence of rotation • Rapid increase of vibrations or buffeting • Hydraulic system loss • Repeated engine stalls
ENG - STALL	THR LEVER IDLE Check engine parameters • If abnormal, ENG SHUTDOWN • If normal: engine anti-ice ON, increase thrust slowly. If a stall occurs, reduce thrust.

ENG - REVERSE UNLOCKED	THR LEVER IDLE • If buffet: speed 240, ENG SHUTDOWN • If REV deployed: full rudder trim towards live engine, control heading with roll. • For APP and LDG: Flap1, VREF+55, 5º rudder towards live engine.
ENG - REVERSE FAULT	THR LEVER IDLE if reverser pressurized. LAND ASAP amber
ENG - ALL ENGINES FAILURE	Might be detected or not by the ECAM. Sometimes only one engine failure is detected (ENG 1(2) FAIL). In case of all engines failure: - RAT automatically deploys - AC ESS SHED and DC ESS SHED bus are on. - Below FL250, APU can be started. Caution must be taken when starting the APU, as each APU start attempt takes around 3 minutes and a half of battery life. See chapter 18 for more information.
ENG FAIL AFTER V1	The T/O must be continued. The procedure is explained in chapter 18.
ENG 1(2) HIGH VIB	If the ECAM alert is triggered, it is just a hint to monitor engine parameters. QRH procedure should be followed.
ENG 1(2) FADEC A(B) FAULT	The alert triggers when one of the associated FADEC channels is lost.
ENG 1(2) FADEC FAULT	Both channels are lost. Engine parameters are lost. Check HYD, BLEED and ELEC pages to monitor engine status. If abnormal, THR IDLE and ENG OFF.

ENG - THRUST LEVER DISAGREE	This triggers when TLA angle sensors are not in agreement. This means that the FADEC does not know the exact TLA angle and therefore cannot produce the exact require thrust. The FADEC gives a fixed theorical value: Ground: Idle if not in TOGA T/O: Take-off thrust Cruise: selects the thrust for the higher TLA detected. APP: idle thrust is selected when slats are selected, even for Go Around.
ENG - THR LEVER FAULT	If a THR lever is failed, it automatically selects IDLE on the GRND. In the air, THR is set to MCT except during T/O until slat retraction, where it freezes at T/O power. Once slats are extended, IDLE is selected (or MN<0.47 if EIU is failed).
ENG - 1(2) LO PR	This triggers when OIL PR> 60 PSI. ENG MASTER SW will be requested OFF. However, if ENG SD indications are LO PR but is not confirmed by the ECAM, it can be assumed that the oil pressure transducer is faulty. ENG can be kept ON monitoring all ENG parameters.

17. MISCELLANOUS

TCAS

The TCAS provides vertical guidance in case of a TCAS RA (Resolution Advisory). The normal TCAS operation is on TA/RA mode. TA should be selected in case of ENG failure, flight with L/G down or airline specific procedures.

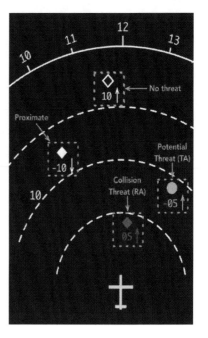

No threat traffic appears as a black diamond, and **proximate traffic** (closer than 6NM or within 1200ft vertically) as a white diamond. **Potential threats** (TAU about 40s) appear in amber, **collision threats** (TAU about 25s) in red. For a TA/RA, pilots have 5s to reach the required V/S (2,5 for corrections).

TCAS is inhibited below 900 ft.

WEATHER RADAR

Weather radar is based on reflectivity of water droplets. Low reflectivity is marked with green, whereas high reflectivity is marked with red. Be aware that the weather radar cannot detected very small particles (fog, some clouds) or weather phenomena with no particles involved at all (e.g. clear air turbulence). In the cruise, it is recommended that the WX radar is set at a **range** of 160 NM on the PM ND, and at a range of 80 NM on the PFD for better situational awareness.

The weather radar **tilt** is dependent on the antenna beam centerline (which is centered using the IRS) and is therefore independent of aircraft pitch and bank angle. Recommended settings are:

- 4º UP for T/O
- 2º DN in the cruise for a range of 80 NM
- 1º DN in the cruise for a range of 160 NM

However, the following formula can be used:

$$h(ft) = d(NM) \times tilt(º) \times 100$$

Where "h" is the difference in height between the aircraft altitude and the radar top altitude. If available, automatic tilt is recommended.

Recommended **safety margins** around a cell are:

- Minimum lateral margin: 20NM
- Minimum distance for decision: 40NM
- Minimum vertical margin: 5000 ft

WINDSHEAR

Windshear is a sudden change in either wind speed or direction, or both, over a short distance. It can be recognized by:

- Airspeed variations in excess of 15 kts
- Wind indication variations
- Vertical speed excursions of 500 ft/min.
- Glide slop deviations of 1 dot.
- Heading variations of 10º

Windshear predictions are computed by the PWS and warnings by the FAC.

The windshear detection function is available:

- At take-off, 3 s after lift off, up to 1 300 ft RA
- At landing, from 1 300 ft RA to 50 ft RA
- With at least CONF1 selected.

Windshear recovery and avoidance are explained in section 18.

OXYGEN

There are two different kinds of oxygen **fixed** systems in an A320:

○ **Cockpit** oxygen: supplied by a high-pressure cylinder. There are generally three full face masks in the cockpit. They all have red grips which must be squeezed together whilst pulling the mask. The <u>emergency</u> selector allows an over-pressure inside the mask in order to eliminate condensation, smoke or smells entering the mask. The <u>100 % selector</u> delivers pure oxygen only (the <u>N</u> selector provides a mixture with cabin air up to a certain ALT).

○ **Cabin** oxygen: supplied via chemical oxygen generators, which supply between 2 and 4 masks each. They provide oxygen for a limited period of time, around an average of 15 minutes.

WATER —38—

Potable water is stored in a 200l tank located in front of the wing box, behind the FWD cargo compartment.

TOILET —38—

Differential pressure forces the waste from the toilet into the waste tank, which has a usable capacity of 170l. Clean water from the potable water system flushes toilets.

CVR

The cockpit voice recorder (CVR) records:

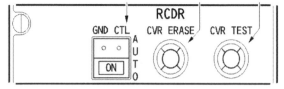

- conversations between crew members in the cockpit
- all aural warnings
- radio communications

- PA messages
- intercommunication between crew members

Only the last 2 hours of conversations are retained. CVR is programmed to stop recording 5 min after ENG shutdown.

When the CVR ERASE P/B (2) is pressed for more than 2 seconds, data is erased if the A/C is on the ground and the parking brake is ON.

FIRE PROTECTION —26—
Engine and APU

They have a fire and overheat detection system including 2 detection loops (A and B) and a fire detection unit (FDU).

The detection loop consists in one sensing element for the APU and the following sensing elements for the engine: pylon nacelle, engine core and engine fan section.

The fire detection will generate a warning if:

- Loops A and B detect fire
- One loop detects fire, the other is faulty
- A break occur in both loops within 5 s of each other.

The APU will auto-shutdown on the ground and the fire extinguisher will be released when a fire is detected (not in flight).

When the **Fire P/B** is released in the overhead panel, the following happens:

- Aural warning is silenced
- Fire extinguisher is armed

Additionally, for the **ENG P/B**:

- Closes LP Fuel Valve and the ENG Bleed.
- Closes the Hydraulic Fire Shut Off Valve and the Pack Flow Ctrl. Valve
- Cuts off the FADEC Supply
- Deactivates the IDG

And for the **APU P/B**:

- Closes the Fuel LP Valve, the APU fuel Pump and the APU Bleed.
- Closes the Xfeed valve and the APU generator.

125

> **TOP TIP!**
>
> The amber "DISCH" light illuminates when pressure is low (the agent has been discharged).

Cargo compartments

The FWD and AFT cargo compartments have 6 smoke detectors: 2 in the FWD compartment and 4 in the AFT compartment. Both compartments share one bottle with two discharge heads, one for each compartment. They are controlled via the SDCU (Smoke Detection Control Unit).

Lavatory and wastebin

Each lavatory has one smoke detector controlled by the SDCU. A signal is seen in the cockpit and in the CIDS.

Each wastebin has an automatic fire extinguishing system.

SMOKE

Smoke is a QRH procedure only except for Avionics smoke, where an ECAM might be generated. If it is generated and smoke is perceptible, follow the ECAM first.

The initial QRH procedure are intended to protect the crew and limit further smoke propagation. Then it will take you through a "Initiate Diversion" bit. The next section (Boxed Items) is a remainder that the Flight Crew may, at any time, refer to the removal of smoke or ELEC EMER CONFIG if needed. The last — longest— part is designed to fight the source of the smoke.

GPWS

The Ground Proximity Warning System generates aural and visual warnings when one of these conditions occurs between 30 and 2450ft. There are 5 different modes:

1. Excessive rate of descent (**"SINK RATE"**, **"PULL UP"**)

2. Excessive terrain closure date (**"TERRAIN"**, **"PULL UP"**)

3. Altitude loss after take off or G/A, if more than 10ft lost after T/O up to 1500ft (**"DON'T SINK"**)

4. Unsafe terrain clearance when not in LDG config. (**"TOO LOW GEAR"**, **"TOO LOW FLAPS"**, **"TOO LOW TERRAIN"**).

5. Too far below G/S (**"GLIDESLOPE"**)

Besides these basic modes, **EGPWS** is an enhanced function that adds:

- TAD (Terrain Awareness Display): Displays terrain on ND

- TCF (Terrain Clearance Floor): Improves low terrain warning during landing.

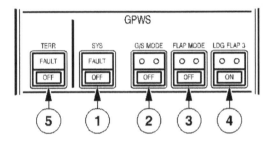

1 - SYS: All GPS basic modes (1 to 5) are inhibited

2 - G/S Mode: G/S mode is inhibited

3 - Flap Mode: "Too low flaps" mode is inhibited

4 - LDG Flap 3: Flap mode inhibited with Flaps 3

5 - Inhibits TAD and TCF modes.

COMMUNICATIONS

Three radio management panels (RMP) and three audio control panels (ACP) control radio communications. The RMPs also provide back up for radio nav aid tuning. Each RMP can tune any communication radio. However, usually RMP1 is dedicated to VHF1, RMP2 to VHF2. A SEL light illuminates when a radio that is not dedicated to that RMP is selected.

The crew can switch to ACP3 if ACP1 or ACP2 fail by using this knob on the overhead panel. When doing this, the third occupant's access to the acoustic system is lost.

See the communications schematics below:

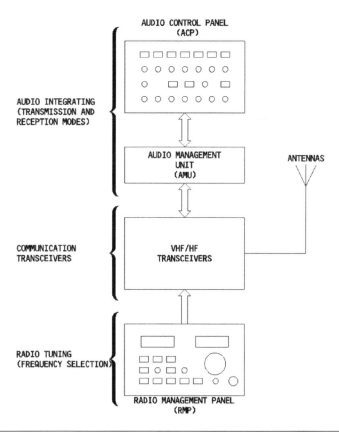

	TOP TIP!

TOP TIP!

Do not operate the HF radio during refuelling.

18. MEMORY ITEMS & PROCEDURES

In this chapter you will find the usual memory items and some procedures that are not officially memory items but could be considered as such. These other procedures are explained at the end of the chapter:

LOSS OF BRAKING

REV .... MAX

BRAKE PEDALS .... RELEASE

A/SKID OFF .... ORDER

A/SKID & N/W STRG .... OFF

BRAKE PEDALS .... PRESS

MAX BRK PR .... 1000 PSI

- **If still no braking**:

PARK BRAKE.. USE

use short successive parking brake applications to stop the aircraft

---

EMERGENCY DESCENT

NOTE: this is the STD Airbus Emergency Descent procedure. For more explanations, refer to Chapter 6 or to your Airline's SOPs (normally a 2 step procedure followed by QRH or ECAM procedure).

CREW OXY MASKS .... USE

SIGNS .... ON

EMER DESCENT .... INITIATE

THR LEVERS.. IDLE (if A/THR not active)

SPD BRK .... FULL

STALL RECOVERY

NOSE DOWN PITCH CONTROL...APPLY

BANK...WINGS LEVEL

- **When out of stall**

THRUST .... INCREASE SMOOTHLY AS NEEDED

SPEEDBRAKES .... CHECK RETRACTED

FLIGHT PATH.. RECOVER SMOOTHLY

- **If in clean configuration and below 20 000 ft**

FLAP1 .... SELECT

STALL WARNING AT LIFT-OFF

Spurious stall warnings may sound and appear on PFD in NORMAL law, if an angle of attack probe is damaged. In this case, apply immediately the following actions:

THRUST.. TOGA

PITCH ATTITUDE 15º

BANK...WINGS LEVEL

UNRELIABLE AIRSPEED INDICATION

If the safe conduct of the flight is impacted:

AP .... OFF

A/THR .... OFF

FD .... OFF

PITCH/THRUST:

< THR RED ALT 15º/TOGA

>THR RED ALT,< FL100.................................... 10º/CLB

>FL100 .... 5º/CLB

if FLAPS 0,1,2,3 .... MANTAIN CURRENT CONFIG

if FLAP FULL .... SELECT CONF3

SPEEDBRAKES .... CHECK RETRACTED

L/G .... UP

- **To level off**

SPEEDBRAKES .... CHECK RETRACTED

PITCH/THRUST TABLE .... APPLY

EGPWS CAUTIONS

"TERRAIN TERRAIN", "TOO LOW TERRAIN", "CAUTION TERRAIN", "CAUTION OBSTACLE"

NIGHT OR IMC

AP .... OFF

PITCH .... PULL UP

THRUST LEVERS .... TOGA

BANK... WINGS LEVEL OR ADJUST

DO NOT CHANGE A/C CONFIGURATION

DAYLIGHT AND VMC

FLIGHT PATH... ADJUST

"SINK RATE"	
ABOVE 1000 ft IMC / 500 ft VMC	FLIGHT PATH ADJUST
BELOW 1000 ft IMC / 5ooft VMC	GO AROUND
"DON'T SINK"	
FLIGHT PATH..	ADJUST
"TOO LOW GEAR" - "TOO LOW FLAPS"	
GO AROUND	PERFORM
"GLIDESLOPE"	
ABOVE 1000 ft IMC / 500 ft VMC	FLIGHT PATH ADJUST
BELOW 1000 ft IMC / 5ooft VMC	G/A CONSIDER
NOTE: when conditions require a deliberate approach below glideslope, set de G/S MODE to OFF.	

EGPWS WARNINGS	
"PULL UP", "TERRAIN AHEAD PULL UP", "AVOID TERRAIN"	
AP	OFF
PITCH	PULL UP
THRUST LEVERS	TOGA
BANK..	WINGS LEVEL OR ADJUST
DO NOT CHANGE CONFIGURATION	

TCAS WARNINGS	
TCAS MODE AVAILABLE	
TRAFFIC ADVISORY ("TRAFFIC")	
TCAS MODE	CHECK ARMED
A/THR	CHECK ON
RESOLUTION ADVISORY	
IF AP ON...	TCAS ACTIONS MONITOR
IF AP OFF..	FD FOLLOW

--

VERTICAL SPEED .... MONITOR

    ⊚   if any "**CLIMB**" message on FINAL APP

TCAS... MONITOR

GO AROUND .... CONSIDER

NOTE: Respect STALL, GPWS and W/S warnings

    ⊚   When "**CLEAR OF CONFLICT**"

AP/FD... MONITOR

ATC... NOTIFY

LATERAL AND VERTICAL GUIDANCE, SPEED .... ADJUST

TCAS MODE NOT AVAILABLE

TRAFFIC ADVISORY ("TRAFFIC")

DO NOT PERFORM ANY MANEUVERS

RESOLUTION ADVISORY

AP .... OFF

FDs .... OFF

VERTICAL SPEED .... ADJUST or MANTAIN

    ⊚   if any "**CLIMB**" message on FINAL APP

GO AROUND .... PERFORM

    ⊚   When "**CLEAR OF CONFLICT**"

AP/FD... MONITOR

ATC... NOTIFY

LATERAL AND VERTICAL GUIDANCE, SPEED .... ADJUST

PREDICTIVE WINDSHEAR

note 1: PWS is computed by the WX radar

note 2: predictive W/S warnings may be disregarded by the flight crew as long as:

- *no signs of possible W/S conditions are visible*
- *reactive W/S system is operational*

However, all W/S reactive warnings must be followed.

TAKE OFF — "WINDSHEAR AHEAD, WINDSHEAD AHEAD"
❧   Before take off: delay T/O
❧   During T/O run: reject T/O (warning inhibited above 100 kt)
❧   When airborne:
THR LEVERS .... TOGA
AP .... KEEP ON
SRS ORDERS .... FOLLOW
If no SRS available, pitch 17,5º initially.
slat/flap configuration might be changed if actual W/S not entered.
LANDING — "GO AROUND, WINDSHEAR AHEAD"
G/A .... PERFORM
AP .... KEEP ON
If no SRS available, pitch 17,5º initially.

REACTIVE WINDSHEAR
note: Reactive W/S is computed by the FAC
"**WINDSHEAR**" message displayed on both PFDs
WINDSHEAR x3 AURAL ALERT
DO NOT CHANGE AIRCRAFT CONFIGURATION
TAKE OFF
BEFORE V1 — REJECT T/O
AFTER V1
THR LEVERS .... TOGA
REACHING VR .... ROTATE
SRS ORDERS .... FOLLOW
AIRBORNE, INITIAL CLIMB OR LANDING
TOGA .... SET OR CONFIRM
AP .... KEEP ON
SRS ORDERS .... FOLLOW

note: Alpha Floor might activate during the maneuver. If this is the case, "TOGA LK" will be active. Once out of the windshear condition, remember to disconnect the A/THR in order to avoid an overspeed situation.

The following procedures are **NOT MEMORY ITEMS**, but they too require immediate actions to be carried by the Flight Crew:

PILOT INCAPACITATION

TAKE CONTROL, RECOVER SAFE FLIGHT PATH

"I HAVE CONTROL" .... ANNOUNCE

PRIORITY P/B .... CONSIDER

AP .... ENGAGE

"MAYDAY" .... DECLARE

ENSURE THE INCAPACITATED PILOT DOES NOT INTERFERE WITH THE HANDLING OF THE A/C. GET HELP FROM THE CABIN CREW IF NEEDED.

ASK FOR A LONG FINAL AND RADAR VECTORS

ENGINE FAILURE AFTER V1

CENTRELINE ....KEEP

AT VR ....ROTATE TO 12,5º

RUDDER TRIM... ADJUST

ABOVE 400 FT:

AP ....CONSIDER

HDG ....PULL

SECONDARY F-PLAN ....REQUEST

Initial ECAM actions should then be conducted. The "MAYDAY" call might be put in at this stage or later depending on airline policy and urgency of such communication. They are completed until one of the following points, at which "ENGINE SECURE" is announced:

- ☜ If no damage — ENG MASTER SW OFF
- ☜ If damage — AG 1 DISCH

@ If damage and fire — AG 2 DISCH

Then "STOP ECAM" should be announced and the flying continued. When above the ONE ENGINE ACC, apply:

V/S 0 ....PUSH

FLAPS .... RETRACT ON SCHEDULE

GREEN DOT... SELECT

OP CLIMB .... SELECT

MCT ....APPLY

Note: if TOGA selected, MAX 10 minutes power available.

ENGINE FAILURE IN THE CRUISE

THRUST LEVERS .... MCT

ATHR... OFF

this avoids the auto-thrust to select IDLE thrust.

STANDARD STRATEGY

SPEED.. M0.78/300kts

REC MAX EO ALTITUDE (PERF CRZ PAGE)............................... ESTABLISH

DESCENT ....INITIATE

V/S .... MIN 500 ft/min

ATHR.. ON

OBSTACLE STRATEGY

SPEED..GREEN DOT

REC MAX EO ALTITUDE (PERF CRZ PAGE)................................... ESTABLISH

MIN SAFE ALTITUDE ....CONSIDER

DESCENT ....INITIATE

once clear of obstacles

STANDARD STRATEGY .... APPLY

Note: SE operations do not support WAI and two packs. If the X-bleed can be opened, WAI available with one pack off.

DUAL ENGINE FAILURE

This procedure is different depending on the situation you are in:

Time to relight — Apply ENG DUAL FAILURE or ALL ENG FAIL <u>QRH</u>.

No time to relight — Apply EMER LANDING <u>QRH</u>.

If time to relight and fuel remaining, the QRH will first ask the F/C to fly above the optimum relight speed (SEE QRH ENG RELIGHT IN FLIGHT) in order to recover one of the engines.

Electric are recovered when APU can be started.

Once recovery is considered impossible, descent at green dot speed is recommended and preparation for the approach is begun.

<u>Profile</u>:

At 280 kt — 2 NM/1000 ft

At Green Dot — 2.5 NM/1000 ft (average rate 1600 ft/min)

At F Speed , L/G DOWN— 1.2 NM/1000 ft

Note: one orbit at GD takes around 4000 ft. Wings level you lose 400ft/nm.

Find a comparison between a 3º glide and a dual engine failure glide with "F" speed and landing gear down:

DISTANCE vs ALTITUDE (APPROACH)

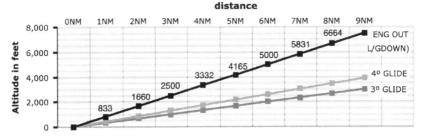

UPSET RECOVERY

The A/C is in an unusual attitude when it has:

- pitch up > 25º
- pitch down >-10º
- bank >45º

- Any flight within these parameters but with inappropriate airspeed.

The next two items are part of the **"upset recovery"** techniques.

NOSE HIGH
AP .... OFF
ATHR.. OFF
PITCH DOWN ....APPLY
THRUST .... ADJUST
BANK..LESS THAN 60º
LEVEL FLIGHT.. RECOVER

NOSE LOW
AP .... OFF
ATHR.. OFF
STALL *(IF APPLICABLE)* ....RECOVER
ROLL... SHORTEST DIRECTION TO WINGS LEVEL
THRUST .... ADJUST
LEVEL FLIGHT ....RECOVER

STANDARD CALLOUTS	
PM CALLOUT	**When parameter exceeds...**
APPROACH PHASE	
SPEED	-5 kt/+10 kt of TARGET SPEED
SINK RATE	1000 ft/min VS
BANK	7º
PITCH	-2,5º / 10º
LOC	1/2 dot LOC
GLIDE	1/2 dot GS
CROSS TRACK	> 0.1 NM of XTK
V/DEV	1/2 dot of vertical deviation (50 ft)
COURSE	1/2 dot, 2,5º (VOR), 5º (ADF)
LANDING PHASE	
PITCH PITCH	7,5º A321 / 10º A320-A319
BANK BANK	7º
GO AROUND PHASE	
BANK	7º
PITCH	If outside +10 and +20º.
SINK RATE	If no climb rate

TAILWIND OR CROSSWIND (>20 kt) TECHNIQUE

1) Set 50% N1 or 1.05 EPR on both engines

2) Apply full forward sidestick

3) Release brakes

4) Rapidly increase thrust to 70 % N1 or 1.15 EPR, then progressively in order to reach take-off thrust by 40 kts.

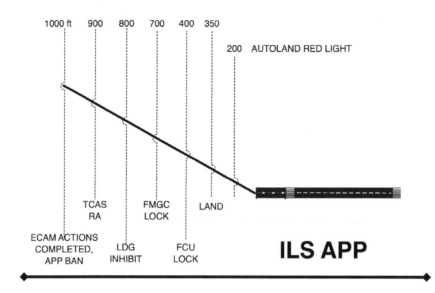

ILS APP

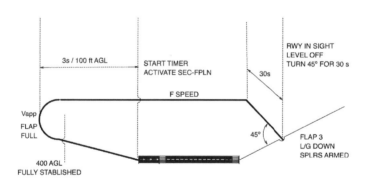

CIRCLING APPROACH

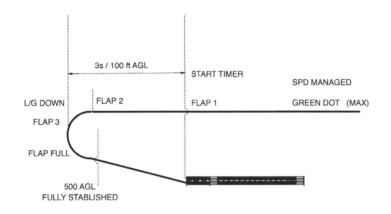

VISUAL APPROACH

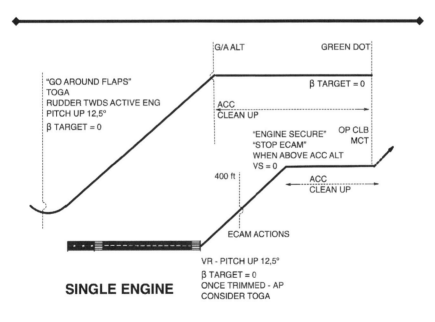

SINGLE ENGINE

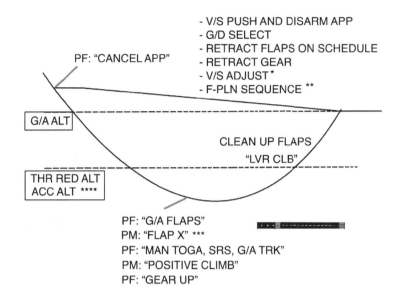

PF: "CANCEL APP"

- V/S PUSH AND DISARM APP
- G/D SELECT
- RETRACT FLAPS ON SCHEDULE
- RETRACT GEAR
- V/S ADJUST*
- F-PLN SEQUENCE **

G/A ALT

CLEAN UP FLAPS
"LVR CLB"

THR RED ALT
ACC ALT ****

PF: "G/A FLAPS"
PM: "FLAP X" ***
PF: "MAN TOGA, SRS, G/A TRK"
PM: "POSITIVE CLIMB"
PF: "GEAR UP"

GO AROUND AND DISCONTINUED APPROACH

DISCONTINUED APPROACH: when flying over the G/A altitude

GO AROUND: when flying below the G/A altitude.

Note: when carrying out a go around very close to the G/A altitude, be prepared to select TOGA and immediately retard the thrust levers back to the CLB detent.

*to achieve desired altitude

**FMGC will lose the active G/A routing if the DEST airport is overflown, or if the A/C flies close to it (less than 7 nm). This is because the FMGC will sequence the F-PLN with the destination airport. In order to avoid this, select a suitable "DIR TO" along the current F-PLN.

***one step up

**** remember that SE operations set ENG OUT ACC/THR RED at the G/A ALT.

CALLS

The following situations have standard callouts or PA calls. You will find the calls next to them. However, you are free to **write your own** in Column 3 if your airline has a different call out.

EGPWS	"PULL UP TOGA"	
TCAS	"TCAS, I HAVE CONTROL"	
STALL	"STALL, I HAVE CONTROL"	
STALL WARN.	"STALL, TOGA 15"	
UNRELIABLE A/S	"UNRELIABLE A/S"	
LOSS OF BRK	"LOSS OF BRAKING"	
RAPID DESCENT	"ATT CREW, RAPID DESC."	
ISSUE ONBOARD	"ATT, CREW AT STATIONS"	
TURBULENCE	"ATT CREW, TURBULENCE"	
N1 TO COCKPIT	"PURSER TO COCKPIT, PLS"	

19. WINTER OPERATIONS AND LOW VISIBILITY

The effect that frozen contamination can have on the aircraft performance on take-off is unpredictable. It is the pilot responsibility to check the following areas before departure:

- Wings, tail and control surfaces
- Fuselage
- Radome and flight deck windows
- Engine inlets, exhaust nozzles, cooling intakes, probes
- Pitot tubes and static ports
- Fuel tank vents
- Landing gear, gear doors and wheel bay
- Air conditioning inlets and outlets

Surface contamination is only permitted by Airbus in the following cases:

- Thin hoar frost on upper fuselage, radome and nacelles
- Less than 3mm of frost on underside of wing tank area.

TOP TIP!

Black triangles mark the best cabin position for wing inspection. On the A320, it is normally the second row forward of the overwing exits.

When taxiing there is a risk that slush might contaminate the **flaps** mechanism. For this reason, flaps are kept retracted until before take-off.

Runway contamination affects the aircraft performance in three ways:

- Lateral control reduced (lateral friction is reduced)
- Stopping capability reduced (longitudinal friction is reduced)
- Contaminant drag reduces acceleration

A runway is said to be contaminated when more of 25 % of the runway area is covered by:

- More than 3 mm of water, slush or loose snow.
- Compacted snow
- Ice

NOTE: slush is water saturated with snow.

When the runway is contaminated with more than:

- 12.7 mm of water or slush
- 25.4 mm of wet snow
- 100 mm of dry snow

Then **take-off** is **prohibited** if. In addition, if there is a layer of contaminant on top of either a compacted snow or ice covered runway do not take off either.

ANTI-ICE

Engine anti-ice must be activated whenever icing conditions are encountered. **Wing** anti-ice must be selected whenever there is an indication of severe ice accumulation on the airframe.

On top of this, pitot tubes, static ports, AOA probes and TAT probes are electrically heated.

DE-ICING/ANTI-ICING FLUID

Several types can be used. Here is a very brief summary:

type 1	type 2,3,4
○ Low viscosity	○ High viscosity
○ Limited hold-over time	○ Longer hold-over time
○ Mainly for de-icing	○ de-icing and anti-icing

The **holdover time** starts from the beginning of the application of the fluid (of the second step if it is a two-step procedure) and depends on the type of fluid and on the nature and severity of the precipitation.

EXAMPLES OF ANTI-ICE PROCEDURES

AEA Type II/75/16.43 local TLS / 19 Dec 99
AEA Type II : Type of fluid used
75   : Percentage of fluid/water mixtures by volume 75% fluid / 25% water
16.43   : Local time of **start** of last application
19 Dec 99   : Date

ISO Type I/50:50/06.30 UTC/ 19 Dec 99
50:50   : 50% fluid / 50 % water
06.30   : Time (UTC) of **start** of last application

TEMPERATURE CORRECTIONS

As you know, temperatures lower than the ISA result in the aircraft flying below the altitude shown by aircraft instruments. This is normally compensated by having some safety margin in the enroute minimum altitudes, and taken into account when being radar vectored.

In the following table you will find a guidance on how to apply temperature corrections to your approach.

	PA 3D (ILS)	APV 3D (RNP VNAV)	2D NPA (RNP LNAV, VOR, NDB, LOC)
When?	Below OATmin		
Limits?	NO	If available, corrections only inside the Chart Tº range.	NO
Where?	Initial* Intermediate* Final Missed APP ---- DA (not DH correction for CATII/III)	Initial* Intermediate* Missed APP	Initial* Intermediate* Final Missed APP --- DA
Mode	LOC G/S	APP NAV	NAV/FPA, TRK/FPA or LOC/FPA (APP NAV not authorized)

*Initial and intermediate segments might be left uncorrected if being radar vectored. If you wish to correct nevertheless, inform ATC.

OATmin is the minimum temperature at which the airline proceduires establish that temperature corrections should begin. OATmin is normally **0ºC** for most airlines.

ENGINE RUN-UPS

In icing conditions, engine run-ups are needed. before take-off on the following conditions:

CFM engines: >70 % power during 30 s at intervals of maximum 30 min.

IAE engines: increase power above 50 % but avoid the 61-74 % range. No specific time for increased power thrust is shown.

LOW VISIBILITY

1000 ft AGL is considered the APP BAN. Instrument approaches may be carried out up to this point even if weather is below minima. However, if the ATC reported conditions fall below minima at or before APP ban, the pilots must go around. Once the A/C flies through APP BAN, final APP might be attempted regardless of the ATC reported weather.

Above 1000 ft, downgrading (triple click) is always possible provided that

- ECAM actions completed
- New minima is inserted
- New briefing performed
- Decision completed before 1000 ft AAL

Conditions that require a go around or reversion to CAT1 between 1000 ft and Alert Height (100 ft):

- A. Engine failure: the aircraft (via the FAC) would trim the aircraft during the G/A if at least one autopilot is engaged.
- B. Downgrading of capability
- C. Loss of AP (cavalry charge)
- D. Alpha floor activation
- E. Amber caution

At 350 ft, "LAND" must be displayed.

At 200 ft or below, any AUTOLAND warning requires a GO AROUND, unless sufficient visual references are obtained. The red autoland light comes on if:

- A. APs lost
- B. Loss of LOC > 15 ft, or GS > 100 ft
- C. RA differ more than 15 ft
- D. FMGS detects a long flare

The failure of LOC or G/S receivers is noticed by their respective scales disappearing, or red LOC or G/S flaps in the PFD.

The failure of LOC or G/S transmitters is noticed by their respective scales flashing, or FD bars flashing.

At flare height, if "FLARE" does not come on the FMA, perform a G/A. If visual references are sufficient, PF may decide to complete the landing.

RVR MEASUREMENTS

RVR measurements are provided by a system of calibrated transmissometers, which are placed at a height between 5 and 10 m above the ground and normally in the following positions:

- TDZ (Touch Down Zone)

- MID (Mid runway portion)

- Stop-end

For continued operations with **failed** or **downgraded** RVR measuring equipment, the following table should be followed:

	TDZ	MID	STP
RVR equipment	Failed	Serviceable*	Failed
failure	Serviceable	Failed	Serviceable**
	Serviceable	Serviceable	Failed

*MID measurements might be used instead of TDZ. However, TDZ minima will apply (see following table)
**Might be disregarded if the A/C is expected to be below 60 kts in that portion of the RWY.

The pilot may assess RVR from the T/O point if the equipment has failed. The crew will then have to count the number of lights they can see on the RWY.

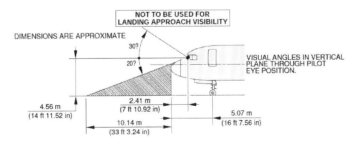

note: notice that the pilots have a blind spot of 12.55 m in front of them.

LOW VISIBILITY MINIMA

CATEGORY	CLOUD BASE	RVR-TDZ	RVR-MID	RVR-STP**
CAT I	>200 ft	>550 m	n/a	n/a
CAT II	100-200 ft	>300 m	75 m (125)*	75 m
CAT IIIa	<100	200 m	75 m (125)*	75 m
CAT IIIb	<50 or no DH	75 m	75 m	75 m

*125 m if manual roll-out only.

**may be disregarded if speed is expected to be below 60 kts in that portion of the runway.

NOTE: Autoland recommended in CAT2 but not mandatory (only CAT3).

NOTE2: check your own <u>airline</u> minima, as it might differ from the table above (you can modify the table yourself!)

VISUAL REFERENCES

- o **CAT II**: 3 consecutive lights: Centre line of APP lights, or TDZ, or RWY Centre Line Lights or RWY edge, or a combination of these. It must include a lateral element: APP lighting crossbar, landing threshold or barrette or the TDZ.
- o **CAT IIIA**: 3 consecutive lights as described above.
- o **CAT IIIB**: One centreline light.

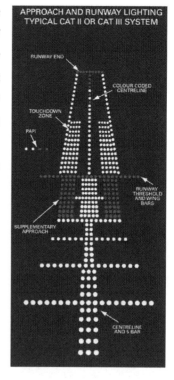

150

<u>LIDO CHARTS</u>: the following items are of key importance when conducting Low Visibility approaches:

Approach Light System category 2 and 3 The first 300m in front of the threshold forms the typical Cat 2 and 3 approach lighting system. It may be combined with any of the below depicted approach systems. ⇒ `Aerodromes General Information` 1 Approach and Runway Lighting Systems	
Approach Light System Abbreviations Identification letter of the approach light system, with intensity (high, medium, low or variable: H, M, L or HL, ML).	
P2: ICAO standard Cat 2 and 3 Approach light system with red side row lights the last 300m/1000ft. Centerline lights white; longitudinal spacing 30m/100ft. Minimum two crossbars located 150m/500ft and 300m/1000ft from THR. The depicted approach lighting system symbols will be used to show all types of approach lighting systems. Specific lighting system variants not affecting the categorization may locally appear.	P2 P2 P2F
Suffix **F**: (P2F, SF, NF) Flashing light unit Indicates that sequenced flashing lights are available (normally from beginning of approach light system to 300m / 1000ft from THR). Each approach light system can be supplemented with sequenced flashing lights.	SF 420
Suffix **R**: (P1R) Flashing RAIL unit Runway alignment indicator lights (RAIL), mainly used in US approach light systems. Instead of barrettes there are sequenced flashing lights available.	P1R
Approach light system length is provided whenever deviating from standard, which is 900m (3000ft) for ICAO, and 2400ft (730m) for U.S. approach light systems.	600
Centerline lights (RCLL) (last 900m-300m / 3000ft-1000ft white/red intermittent, last 300m-0m / 1000ft-0ft red).	
Centerline lights (RCLL) **spacing** and light intensity (high, medium, low or variable: H, M, L or HL, ML). See Lights, Visual Aids, Arresting Systems for details.	15 HL
Centerline lights all white (other non-standard coloring is specified with additional text).	
Runway Touchdown Zone Lights (RTZL), standard 900m / 3000ft.	

20. COMPLEX ROUTES

OCEANIC AIRSPACE

Most of the oceanic airspace in the North Atlantic region is designated as NAT HLA (North Atlantic High Level Airspace) between FL285 and FL420. Additionally, this airspace is RVSM airspace.

CAUTION! This airspace was previously described as "NAT MNPS".

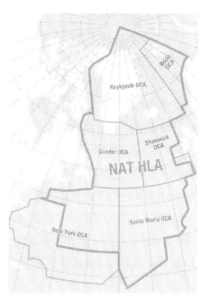

Position reporting

Normally at every waypoint inside the NAT HLA.

- @ Callsign and frequency
- @ Position and Time
- @ FL
- @ Next Position and ETA
- @ Subsequent Position and ETA

"POSITION; MONARCH ONE ZERO ONE TWO, ON FREQUENCY EIGHT EIGHT TWO FIVE, GONAN AT ZERO SIX ONE FIVE, FLIGHT LEVEL THREE NINE ZERO, ESTIMATING EKROK ZERO SIX FIVE EIGHT, NEXT NAXIX AT ZERO SEVEN THREE FIVE"

Position reports are normally preceded by a message like:

"(OCA), MONARCH ONE ZERO ONE TWO, on 8825, POSITION, OVER"

And the OCA will give you a "go ahead" before your position report.

Oceanic Clearance Request

It has to obtained before entering Oceanic Airspace as specified in the cases specified below. It has to include:

- @ ATC Call-Sign

@ ETA & Point of Entry into OCA

@ Request Cruising Mach Number

@ Request FL and the next acceptable higher level

"SHANWICK RADIO, REQUEST OCEANIC CLEARANCE, MONARCH 0879, ESTIMATING LASNO AT ZERO FIVE THREE ZERO. REQUEST MACH DECIMAL SEVEN EIGHT, FLIGHT LEVEL THREE FOUR ZERO, ABLE FLIGHT LEVEL THREE SIX ZERO"

And a clearance example:

"SHANWICK, MONARCH 0879 IS CLEARED TO BEGAS VIA T9. FROM LASNO MAINTAIN FLIGHT LEVEL THREE FOR ZERO, MACH DECIMAL SEVEN ERIGHT"

Selcal checks

All A/C with HF also have a Selcal system. Upon receiving a call code corresponding to that of the A/C, the SELCAL system aurally and verbally advises the Flight Crew that a station is calling. The CALL legend of the HF1 transmission key will flash amber and a buzzer will sound.

Example below:

"MONARCH 590, REQUEST SELCAL TEST ON 8825"

Upon receiving Selcal:

"MONARCH 590, SELCAL TEST OK" or "NEGATIVE SELCAL, TRY AGAIN".

Frequencies

HF frequencies can be found at LIDO GENERAL COM. VHF Frequencies for Oceanic Clearances can be obtained by ATC.

Strategic Lateral Offset Procedure (SLOP)

An strategic lateral offset not exceeding 2nm right of centre-line provide an additional safety margin against wake turbulence encounters from other A/C. This is applicable in the Reykjavik and Shanwick Oceanic CTA above FL285 and does not require ATC clearance.

SLOP should be applied after OCA entry and removed before exit.

T9

(LASNO-BEGAS) is the most commonly used route to/from Spain and the Canary Islands and Northern Europe.

Southbound: Oceanic CLR requests to Shanwick Radio on VHF, 127.65m a maximum of 90 mins before entry and a minimum of 30 minutes before Oceanic boundary, or as soon as possible. Set transponder to 2000 at least 10 minutes after passing LASNO.

Northbound: Oceanic CLR requests to Shanwick Radio on HF, at least 30 minutes before BEGAS. Set transponder to 2000 10 minutes after passing BEGAS.

T213

Airway T213 is less common but very similar to T9. Relevant points are TAMEL (Southbound) and BERUX (Northbound).

T13/T16

Southbound (T16): Oceanic Clearance request to Shanwick Radio on VHF or HF. Southbound flights on T16 will receive the Oceanic Clearance with full details until NAVIX, or possibly a waypoint further. There is no requirement to get an extra clearance from Santa Maria before reaching GONAN. Set the transponder to 2000 30 min after OMOKO.

Northbound (T13): Oceanic Clearance request to Santa Maria Radio on VHF frequency or HF, 40 minutes before MANOX, or as soon as possible after departure. As with the Southbound case, there is no need to get a reclearance after passing GONAN.

OPERATION TO ICELAND

There are a few routes connecting the United Kingdom and Iceland. All of them require HF coverage except the RATSU-BARKU route.

North/Westbound: for routes via ATSIX or GOMUP, Oceanic Clearance request to Shanwick only 40 min before the boundary point. NON-HF equipped A/C flying via BARKU will request Oceanic Clearance from Reykjavik at least 20 minutes before BARKU.

South/Eastbound: All clearances are taken on the ground. For routes to ATSIX or GOMUP. a selcal check must be performed before entering Shanwick Oceanic Airspace.

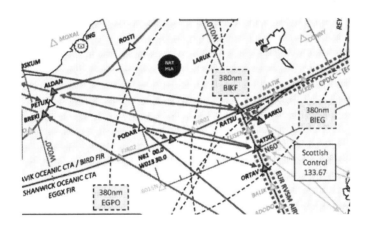

OPERATION TO AFRICA

One of the main characteristics of the Africa Region is the lack of communications, or communications which are not reliable. For that reason there is a designated frequency (126.9) used for pilot broadcasts across specific FIRs, described below:

Some IFRs do have CPDLC connection. In mid-2020 these FIR are Niamey FIR, N'Djamena FIR and Brazzaville FIR.

Broadcasts should be performed:

- 10 min before entering an FIR region
- Upon entering the FIR region
- As soon as practicable after departure from an aerodrome within the region
- 10 minutes before joining an ATS route or crossing a waypoint
- Before a change in FL
- Upon reaching the designated FL
- Apart from that, at least every 20 minutes or whenever the pilot considers.

However, if various of these conditions are met almost together, pilot can exercise their right not to make that many broadcasts.

Broadcasts should be made as follows:

"ALL STATIONS,

THIS IS MONARCH 7637 IN THE (OAC) FIR

POSITION... AT .... FL .... BOUND....

ON... (AIRWAY)..., ESTIMATING.... AT ....

.... NEXT"

Pilot should adhere to their FL and the use of the SLOP procedure is highly recommended. Transponder will be set to 2000 and the use of TCAS is in TA/RA is advised.

Once the A/C approaches its destination, if it is under no ATC control, contact the relevant TWR/APPR control around 20-30 minutes before arrival.

COMPLEX AIRPORTS

In the following pages you will see a few gotcha's that you will find in your day-to-day operations. They have airport specific examples but they could be found anywhere!

VOR Gotcha's (LEAL)

One airport, one approach, two VORs. And both of them far from the RWY threshold. Caution must be taken in order to fly the APP with the correct VOR reference.

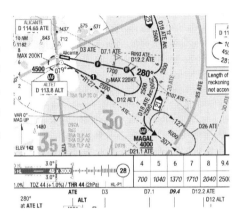

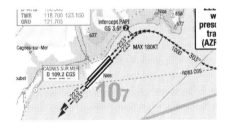

VISUAL restrictions (LFMN)

Many airports have many restrictions when flying visually. Make sure you read them before carrying out a visual approach!

BUMPY ROAD (LFRS)

Careful with irregular profiles like the one in Nantes, Bristol or Leeds. Read the charts!

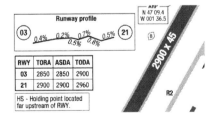

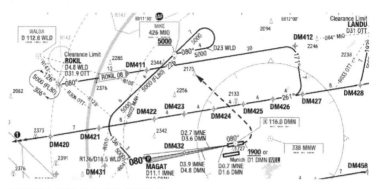

AROUND AND AROUND (EDDM)

This is an APPR onto EDDM, but this can be found in many places, especially in Germany. APPR transitions are endless "S" shaped routes. You should prepare for a good shortcut.

3.40° **D KFN** **143°** RWY 142°		7.5	7	6	5	(14)	⬁3.0° **2436 x 45**
		2400	2200	1850	1490		32 / 1hPa TDZ ---

PAPI's DISCREPANCY (LGKF)

This is the VOR14 APPR in CORFU. As you can see, it is a 3.40º descend, but with a PAPI set a 3º. That means that, once you go visual, you might find yourself with 3 whites.

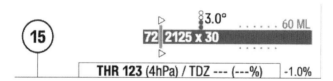

RUNWAY WIDTH (LGSR)

Pay attention to the (2125 x **30**)!

When passing 1000, contact Lisbon APP. Report only passing altitude.

		120	150	180	210	240	270
	GS	120	150	180	210	240	270
6.0%	ft/MIN	800	1000	1100	1300	1500	1700

AUTOMATIC FREQUENCY CHANGES (LPPT)

LISBON is just one example. Barcelona (LEBL) just changed too for instance!

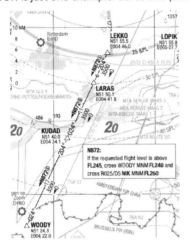

SID/STAR RESTRICTIONS (EHAM)

Be careful when ready the SID/STAR plates, even the "continuation" ones. There is vital information in them. As an example, EHAM has a restriction to pass WOODY at FL240 or above in some SIDs, which is actually sometimes forgotten.

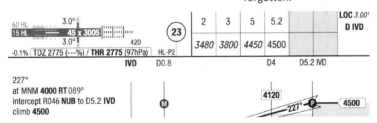

HIGH ALTITUDE AWARENESS! (LEVD)

ILS Platform altitude 4500 ft. It seems high, but airport altitude is 2775! So you are less than 2000 ft AGL (and therefore, you probably should be already at F2 and maybe L/G down before or at G/S interception!

CLEARANCE LIMITS (EGKK)

Establish you clearance limit point and ensure the A/C will not fly through it automatically without CLR form ATC. One good example is Gatwick and the approach via Willo. Your FMS will probably have a loop in Willo (not a hold!) and continue towards the ILS, which is —most likely— not what ATC wants you to do!

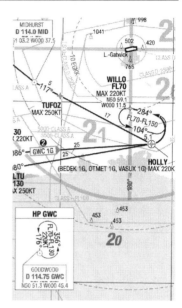

Warning

Do not proceed beyond WILLO without ATC clearance

LOCAL WEATHER PHENOMENA (GCTS)

Some airports have very specific WX phenomena. For instance, GCTS have occasional WS on finals due to the Teide being very close to the APP path.

Of course they are not usually in the plates, so experience is of relevant importance here!

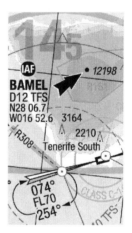

160

OFFSET APPROACH (LIRP)

See how the APP is flown with track 203º but RWY TRK is 214º.

Found at many airports, be cautious and brief what you expect when going visual.

RUNWAY INCURSIONS (LFPG)

Just one example. Situational awareness is of vital importance!

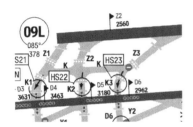

RNAV PROFILE IN FMGS (LFMN)

RNAV APPs draw a G/S like vertical profile from the FAF (like the dotted line in the picture). Therefore, in some cases, FMGC altitudes before the FAF might not be coincident with your chart. If you press the APP button too early, the A/C might even want to climb (for instance, at BISBO) in order to intercept the FMGC profile!

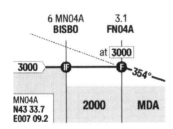

21. FAILURE MANAGEMENT AND SCENARIOS

Failure management takes a key role in your training as a pilot and in your whole career as a flight crew. Remember the **Airbus golden rules,** which take vital importance during an emergency, especially at the onset:

FLY: fly the aircraft, monitor your flight path and your energy. Check your FMAs. Is everything behaving as you expected? Are you using the right levels of automation? Any intervention needed? If automation was lost, can your recover it?

KEEP CALM AND AVIATE, NAVIGATE, COMMUNICATE

NAVIGATE through your flight plan and be aware of terrain (MSA). Any deviations required?

COMMUNICATE with ATC only if extremely necessary to do so. Put a PAN/MAYDAT call in if time is appropriate and you need to do so at this stage. If interrupted, you can always put a standby call:

"Monarch 087T, climb level 240"

"Standby, Monarch 087T".

With Cabin Crew if immediate hidden information might be necessary. If you heard a loud bang and nothing appears in the ECAM, maybe they know more? Any PA calls needed? (*"Attention, crew at stations"*)

So when a **Master Warning** (red) or a **Master Caution** appear, the first thing the PF will say is:

"I have control"

And instead of instantly being driven into the ECAM, he-she will first go through the "fly, navigate, communicate", procedure. Take a breath, do not overreact to the new status of the aircraft and, if appropriate, go through all the steps out loud. Verbalizing what goes through your mind in those stressing seconds will help overcoming the shock. Something like this...

"MASTER CAUTION, I HAVE CONTROL. AP2, ATHR is ON. FMA, SPEED ALT. WE ARE NAVIGATING ON THE SID AND MSA IS 5000 FT."

will share your mental picture too and be a good start in order to start your ECAM actions.

From this point onwards, every airline treats the situation in a different way. Some of them start with an introductory "read ECAM", some get you immediately sucked into the problem with an "ECAM actions", maybe accompanied with a "I have control and communications, ECAM actions". Your airline manuals will describe how they want you to perform the ECAM actions. However, here is an example of an ECAM management for a given failure:

PF	PM
First pilot who notices	
MASTER WARNING/CAUTION .... RESET	
	TITLE ....ANOUNCE
	ECAM ....CONFIRM
OEB..CONSIDER	
CALL "MY RADIOS" "ECAM ACTIONS" ....ORDER	
	ECAM ACTIONS ....PERFORM
	"CLEAR (system)?" ....REQUEST
"CLEAR (system)"................ CONFIRM	
	CLR PB .... PRESS
For each System Display Page	
SD PAGE..ANALYZE	
	"LAND ASAP (RED/AMBER)" ...... READ

163

	"CLEAR (system)?" .... REQUEST
"CLEAR (system)" .... CONFIRM	
When Status Page Appears	
"STOP ECAM" ....ORDER	"STATUS" ....ANNOUNCE ECAM ACTIONS ....STOP
	NORMAL OR EXPANDED C/L, SYSTEM RESET...CONSIDER
"CONTINUE ECAM" ....ORDER	
	STATUS.. READ
	"REMOVE STATUS?" .... REQUEST
"REMOVE STATUS" .... CONFIRM	
	"ECAM ACTIONS COMPLETED"

Of course, and as explained before, your airline might have different procedures. For instance, some airlines include the OEB consideration during the Status phase.

Failures are displayed as you can see in the diagram below.

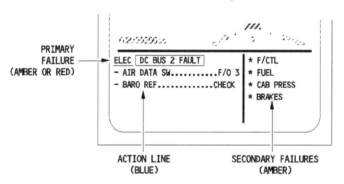

As you can see, primary failures are boxed. This means that this failure affects other systems, which are listed next to them (secondary failures).

When going through the ECAM, read until the next <u>UNDERLINED</u> item (not boxed one!) or until the first one is finished. For instance, when dealing with the picture above you would get to the end and say:

CLEAR ELEC?

CLEAR ELEC

DECISION MAKING PROCESS

Once the ECAM actions have been completed, it is time to proceed to the next stage. *WHAT DO WE DO?*

Different systems have been designed to help the pilots throughout the process. Your airline will choose which one to use. The most common ones are DODAR (and T-DODAR) and FORDEC:

T- Time How *much time do I have?*	**F** - Facts *What do I have?*
D - Diagnose *What do I have?*	**O** - Options
O - Options *Where can I go?*	**R** -- Risks *(and Benefits)*
D - Decide	**D** Decide
A - Assign *tasks to each pilot*	**E** - Execution, *and who does what*
R - Review *Brief, Status...*	**C** - Check

As you can see, both systems are very similar. Please take into account that —in both of them— the time factor is extremely important. With some failures we have all the time we need. With others (fuel leak, emer config...) simply we do not. So in these cases, the crew will have to prioritize.

When presenting all factors and balancing out the benefit/risk of each option, some pilots use more acronyms in order to help them run the diagnosis and options bit. There are a few of them:

<u>WOLF</u> — Weather, Operational, Landing Distance, Fuel

<u>SWIPE</u> — Suitability, Weather, Instrument (APP)? Performance, Endurance

So when beginning your decision making process, one of the options above (or another one) will help you gather all the information you need, and apply the correct level of agility to the process (Endurance-Fuel considerations).

NON-TECHNICAL SKILLS (NOTECHs)

During your assessments —not only in the simulator— you will be assessed by your technical and non-technical skills. NOTECHs are becoming more and more important every day:

- Decision Making: good diagnosis, option generation.
- Situational Awareness: system and environment awareness
- Leadership: use of assertiveness, workload management.
- Teamwork: include others in you decision making, delegate.
- Communication: be clear, supportive.

V_{APP} CALCULATION

Although nowadays this is mostly achieved through the EFB, here you will find some diagrams about V_{app} calculations without and with failure:

W(1000KG)	40	44	48	52	56	60	64	68	72	76	78
VLS CONF FULL (KT)	106	111	116	121	125	130	134	138	142	146	148
VLS CONF 3 (KT)	110	115	120	125	130	135	139	143	147	151	153

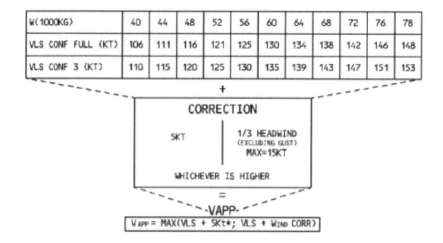

$$+$$

CORRECTION

| 5KT | 1/3 HEADWIND (EXCLUDING GUST) MAX=15KT |

WHICHEVER IS HIGHER

$$=$$

VAPP

$$V_{APP} = MAX(VLS + 5Kt*;\ VLS + W_{IND}\ CORR)$$

W(1000Kg)	40	44	48	52	56	60	64	68	72	76	78
VREF=VLS CONF FULL	106	111	116	121	125	130	134	138	142	146	148

+

△VREF

+

WIND CORRECTION	
△VREF ≥ 20KT	△VREF < 20KT
NO WIND CORRECTION	1/3 HEADWIND (△VREF + WIND CORR LIMITED TO 20KT)

=

VAPP

$$V_{APP} = V_{REF} + \triangle V_{REF} + WIND\ CORR$$

TO BE INSERTED ON MCDU PERF APPR PAGE

FUEL PENALTY FACTORS

Remember that any failure impacting the fuel consumption will make the FMS fuel predictions unreliable, except for the OEI condition.

The following formulae should be used in order to calculate our trip penalty:

Single failure: (FOB - EFOB) x FPF

Multiple failures: (FOB - EFOB) x (FPF1+FPF2+...)

SCENARIOS

You will be aware that your OPC/LPC/LOE assessments will be full of failures that you will be facing in the 2-3-4 h slot assigned to you. You might be aware too that pilots are normally presented with 3 single failures each, all of them with a different level of difficulty. The following tables gives examples according to the difficulty of the failure:

Level 1	Level 2	Level 3
TCAS RA	Sick passenger	Flaps locked
MEL - ADR 2 INOP	A/THR fail in cruise	Fuel leak
MEL - Cargo Door Open indication	MEL - Single FMGC inop at dispatch	Rapid depressurization
CDL - Landing light lens missing	Dangerous goods incident	Tyre debris found on the RWY
ND fail	NWS fault	Dual ADR fault
NPA	Loss of GREEN HYD	Cargo smoke
RFFS Downgrade	FMGC 1 failure	Loss of communications
DMC 2 Fault	W/S on APP	Dual HYD failure

Do not be an ECAM-driven person, because ECAM (or even the QRH) is not always right or will not always tell you the right course of action. Hence it is very important that you have a good A/C knowledge.

Let's see some examples in which the ECAM will not solve your problems, or actually, it will make them worse!

    A.   Engine fire and engine failure: a very typical scenario. Imagine you have multiple bird strikes. One engine fails, the other one does not but it catches fire. The ECAM does always give priority to warnings, hence the fire will be coming up first. Do you remember the ECAM procedure in case of ENG fire? Exactly! Shut down the ENG. Would you do that when the other one has failed too?

B.   You have a CAB SYS 1+2 Fail, but at low level. You decide not to continue and carry out the ECAM actions. On top of that, the Outflow Valve has failed closed and the Cabin Pressure starts to rise very quickly. You decide to refer to the Cabin Overpressure QRH. which tells you to select either Pack 1 or 2 OFF. You do that, but it actually does not do much. Why? This is because the procedure is designed to happen at high altitudes. If you continue down the QRH procedure you will see a "10 min before landing", asking to turn both packs off. This is what should be followed at low altitudes. The 10 min before landing is just a prompt to turn both packs off at low level. Of course, the QRH does not mention it anywhere!

C.   A double FWC fail would be unnoticed as no ECAM would be generated from that point onwards. If you suspect double FWC failure, perform a fire test and see whether an ECAM is generated.

22. WALK AROUND

The A320 walk around and the order that should be followed is described in many documents so it is not our intention to go through that entirely. However, key or commonly forgotten items are described below. After this, you will find schematics of the A320 antennas and panels so that you can have a good knowledge of them when doing your walk around:

Check that the parking brake light is illuminated in the Nose Landing Gear.

Pitot tubes, TAT probes and static ports: check that they are not damaged or have any obstructions.

Crew oxygen overboard discharge indicator in place, otherwise it is an indication that there has been an overpressure in the crew oxy

Hydraulic or any other **leaks**: check that there is no leaks, especially near the landing gear or under the A/C.

Pay special attention to the engine fan cowl latches. They must be properly closed.

Ensure that all safety pins are removed

Of course, look for any missing rivets or loose bolts.

In the tail, check that the APU fire extinguisher disc (red) is in place.

171

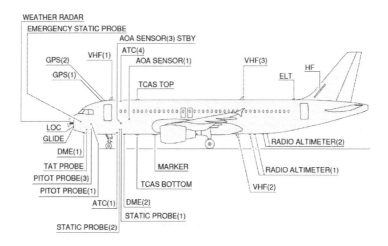

WEATHER RADAR
EMERGENCY STATIC PROBE
AOA SENSOR(3) STBY
ATC(4)
AOA SENSOR(1)
GPS(2) VHF(1)
GPS(1)
TCAS TOP
VHF(3)
HF
ELT
LOC
GLIDE
DME(1)
RADIO ALTIMETER(2)
TAT PROBE
MARKER
PITOT PROBE(3)
RADIO ALTIMETER(1)
PITOT PROBE(1)
TCAS BOTTOM
VHF(2)
ATC(1) DME(2)
STATIC PROBE(1)
STATIC PROBE(2)

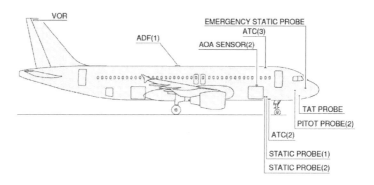

VOR
EMERGENCY STATIC PROBE
ATC(3)
ADF(1)
AOA SENSOR(2)
TAT PROBE
PITOT PROBE(2)
ATC(2)
STATIC PROBE(1)
STATIC PROBE(2)

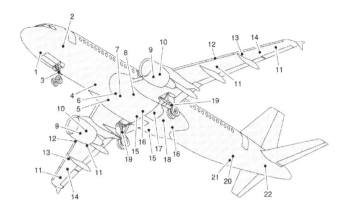

1 – GROUND ELECTRICAL POWER
    CONNECTOR
2 – OXYGEN SYSTEM
3 – NLG GROUNDING (EARTHING) POINT
4 – POTABLE WATER DRAIN PANEL (OPTIONAL)
5 – POTABLE WATER DRAIN PANEL
6 – LOW PRESSURE AIR PRE–CONDITIONING
7 – HIGH PRESSURE AIR PRE–CONDITIONING
8 – REFUEL/DEFUEL INTEGRATED PANEL
9 – IDG/STARTER OIL SERVICING
10 – ENGINE OIL SERVICING
11 – OVERPRESSURE PROTECTOR
12 – REFUEL/DEFUEL COUPLINGS
    (OPTIONAL–LH WING)

13 – OVERWING REFUEL (IF INSTALLED)
14 – NACA VENT INTAKE
15 – YELLOW HYDRAULIC–SYSTEM SERVICE PANEL
16 – BLUE HYDRAULIC–SYSTEM SERVICE PANEL
17 – ACCUMULATOR CHARGING (GREEN SYSTEM)
    AND RESERVOIR DRAIN (GREEN SYSTEM)
18 – GREEN HYDRAULIC–SYSTEM SERVICE PANEL
19 – MLG GROUNDING (EARTHING) POINT
20 – WASTE WATER SERVICE PANEL
21 – POTABLE WATER SERVICE PANEL
22 – APU OIL SERVICING

23. DANGEROUS GOODS AND EMERGENCY EQUIPMENT

DANGEROUS GOODS

Dangerous goods are items that may endanger the safety of an aircraft or persons onboard the aircraft. Their carriage onboard aircrafts is governed by:

- o ICAO, Annex 18. DOC 9284.
- o IATA
- o Local regulations (in Europe, EU 965/2012)
- o Airline manuals (OMA)

From a general rule, the transportation of dangerous goods is forbidden. Some airlines do, however, have permission to transport dangerous goods.

Even if the airline does not have that permission, dangerous can be found in an A/C because they might be hidden dangerous goods (Car parts, for instance) or because they can be carried in minimal quantities (alcohol).

Some dangerous goods that are not permitted may be carried (see Table 2.3.A in the IATA regulations), and they come in three groups: let's see some examples.

- • <u>Group 1</u>: with operator's approval and PIC notification —like wheelchairs with spillable batteries.

- <u>Group 2</u>: operator's approval — like dry ice (not above 2 kg), small gaseous oxygen or air cylinders required for medical use, wheelchairs or other battery-powered mobility aids with non spillable batteries.

<u>Group 3</u>: no approval — like alcoholic beverages (under 5l per receptacle, 24-70 % by volume, max 5l per person) or small clinical thermometers for instance.

EMERGENCY AND. CABIN EQUIPMENT

<u>CIDS — Cabin Intercommunication Data System</u>
Processes signals for many different services: interphones, PAs, reading lights, cabin illumination, lavatory smoke detectors, emergency evacuation signaling... It is controlled via the **FAP** (Flight Attendant Panel).

<u>ACP.— Area call panel</u>
Located in pairs along the cabin ceiling and permit the crew identify where the call is coming from, as well as the nature of the call. It has three different colours:

- o   Blue: call from PAX seat
- o   Red: Normal Crew call, if <u>flashing</u>, emergency call
- o   Amber: call from lavatory, if <u>flashing</u>, smoke in lavatory.

<u>AIP — Attendant Indication Panel</u>
Panels located next to the CC stations and provides the CC with additional relevant information about the event provided by the CIDS. There are 2 lights: flashing red for emergency and steady green for normal operation.

<u>COCKPIT EMERGENCY EQUIPMENT</u>
Fire Extinguiser, Oxygen Bottle, Axe, Medical Kit, Escape Ropes, Life Vest, Flash Lights.

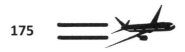

DOOR OPERATION

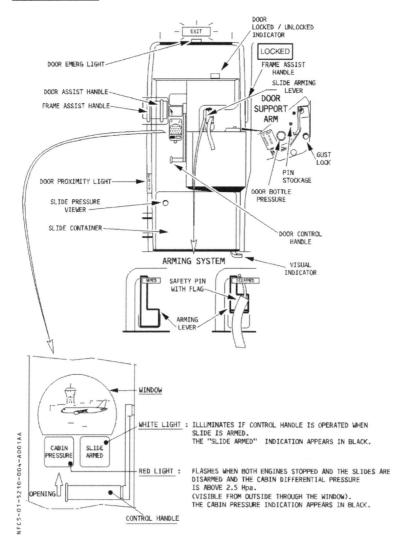

PORTABLE OXYGEN

O2

bottles are available throughout the cabin. They have one or two masks each. They have a capacity of 310 litres, with a High (HI) rate of 4 litres per minute, or a Low (LO) rate of 2 litres per minute.

PBE — PROTECTIVE BREATHING EQUIPMENT

PBE l'Air Liquide
15 minutes
O₂ gaseous
Activation: placing the hood

PBE Dräger
15 minutes
Chemical O₂
Activation: deep breathing or by pulling the quick starter.

24. OEB

OEBs are issued to rapidly inform operators of any deviation from initial design objectives that have a significant operational impact. OEBs can be:

RED: non-compliance may have a significant impact on the safe operation of the aircraft

WHITE: non-compliance may have a significant impact on the operation of the aircraft

OEB36	**No SRS engagement during G/A in the case of EPR Mode Fault**
	When engines are in N1 control mode (EPR control mode inoperative), go-around mode does not engage. The aircraft reverts to basic guidance V/S-HDG or FPA-TRK with pitch down indications. AP might disengage.
	Procedure:
	GO-AROUND .... ANNOUNCE
	AP .... OFF
	FDs .... OFF
	MANUAL GO AROUND .... PERFORM
	When appropriate
	FD .... ON
	APPROPIATE VERTICAL AND LAT MODES................................... USE
	AP .... CONSIDER
OEB41	**Erroneous Alternate Fuel Predictions upon modification of a Company Route in the Alternate Flight Plan**
	When the flight crew modifies the CO RTE in the ALTN F-PLN, the FMS no longer computes the ALTN fuel predications.
	Procedure:
	ENTER manually a waypoint in the en-route F-PLN to start a new computation. Then maintain this point or delete it.

OEB42	**Incorrect Vertical Profile During Non-Precision Approaches**
	This is triggered when the vertical profile before the FAF computed by the FMS is not consistent with the chart vertical profile. As a result, the erroneous vertical profile may consist in a descent segment followed by a level off at the altitude constraint coded at the FAF.
	Procedure:
	If:
	o The operator has established a list of affected NPAs and the procedure is IN the list, OR
	o The procedure contains two or more FPA between the descent point and the MAP/RWY/FAP, AND
	o There is an AT OR ABOVE constraint coded at the FAF:
	MANAGED LATERAL AND VERTICAL......................... AVAILABLE
	if:
	o The operator has established a list of affected NPAs and the procedure is NOT IN the list, or
	o Codings listed above are not used.
	SELECTED VERTICAL GUIDANCE .... USE
	VDEV SYMBOL... DISREGARD
	LNAV/VNAV minima.. DO NOT USE
OEB46	**No engagement of guidance mode**
	If the RA transmits an erroneous height indication, one of the following might happen:
	o After T/O: NAV mode not engaged
	o During G/A: SRS and GA-TRK engage, but NAV, HDG or TRAK modes cannot be selected, LVR CLB is not displayed and ALT* will not engage.
	Procedure
	AP .... OFF

FD .... OFF THEN ON

Aircraft reverts to basic modes

AUTOMATION .... RE-ENGAGE

For the following approach:

G/S MODE .... DO NOT USE

| OEB47 | **HYD ENG PUMP LO PR followed by HYD RSVR OVHT** |

Fluid leakage from the green or yellow hydraulic systems might cause the PTU to operate at high speed due to its inability to pressurize the affected system. If this happens, the reservoir of the other hydraulic system might overheat.

Procedure:

if:

HYD X ENG 1/2 PUMP LO PR ECAM, followed by

HYD Z RSVR OVHT ECAM

(where "X" is G/Y system with LO PR, and "Z" the opposite):

PTU .... OFF

Z ENG PUMP .... KEEP ON

| OEB48 | **Abnormal V Alpha Prot** |

In normal law, if two or three OAO probes are blocked at the same angle value, an increase in the Mach number may result in the activation of the high Angle-of-Attack protection.

Procedure:

If any of the following happens:

o   Alpha Max strip hides completely the Alpha Prot strip in wings-level stabilized flight.

o   Alpha Prot strip rapidly moves by more than 30 kts during flight maneuvers with AP ON

o   Continuous nose down pitch rate that cannot be stopped with backward sidestick:

	ONE ADR .... KEEP ON
	TWO ADRS .... OFF
OEB54	**Incorrect FAC Weight due to dash CG on FUEL PRED page**
	Caused. by an invalid CG in the FMS, which causes the FAC to compute characteristic speeds with the latest GW used, which value might differ a lot with the current and real weight. This is noticed by a dashed CG in the FUEL PRED page.
	Procedure:
	AFTER ENGINE START:
	CG on FUEL PRED page (FMS1 or 2) .... CHECK
	if GW CG dashed, ZFWCG value .... ENTER
	CG on FUEL PRED page .... CHECK
OEB57	**Speedbrake limitation in approach with GWCG above 35% or in overweight landing**
	During descent preparation, if GWCG above 35 % (check FUEL PRED page), or in overweight landing conditions, speedbrake limitation applies:
	AT OR BELOW 240KT: DO NOT USE SPEEDBRAKE
	If deceleration rate not sufficient, consider landing gear extension.

25. YOUR NOTES

This chapter is designed for **you**. Its main use is to allow you to take your notes from your SIM sessions in order to learn from your mistakes for the next one. However, it may be used for any other reason (further explanations, items not covered in this book...)

your notes...

your notes...

your notes...

your notes...

Made in the USA
Columbia, SC
18 August 2024

40682586R00102